THE AMISH YEAR

Text by Rollin C. Steinmetz
Photographs by Charles S. Rice

This charming and informal
book describes and illustrates typical incidents in an ordinary year of
work and play among the Amishmen of Lancaster County, Pennsylvania. Here are the Amish
engaged in the everyday activities
of country life — working hard on
their rich farms, shrewdly doing
business in town, relaxing at a
wedding or a barn-raising, soberly
attending a funeral. We see the
ways in which they are enough like
us to be the family next door. We
see, too, the ways in which they
are different — the old-fashioned
cut of their clothes, the simplicity
of their homes, their refusal to
use electricity or motor-powered
vehicles, their evasion of publicity,
their aversion to modern habits.

Here and there, as the authors
make plain, modernity is creeping
in upon this distinctive way of life,
but the Amish still preserve a stable
and healthy society.

Although the Amish do not
care to be either photographed or
written about, Mr. Rice and Mr.
Steinmetz, as neighbors of long
standing, have succeeded in por-
traying them in a series of casual,
vivid photographs and verbal
sketches.

The
AMISH YEAR

The
AMISH YEAR

CHARLES S. RICE

•

ROLLIN C. STEINMETZ

RUTGERS UNIVERSITY PRESS

New Brunswick *New Jersey*

The Amish Year

The
AMISH YEAR

Who Are the Amish?

Most Americans know a little about the Amish. They're stern. They're quaint. They own no automobiles, use no electricity. Their clothes, fastened with hooks and eyes instead of buttons, are of antique style. They speak Pennsylvania Dutch.

But who are they, really? Why has an America enmeshed in the complexities of modern living "taken up" the Amish like a new toothpaste? For there is a real vogue for the Amish. They have made their appearance in two musical shows, one performed in Lancaster, Pennsylvania, and then in an off-Broadway theater, the other a large success on Broadway and on the road and in England and finally in summer stock. They have been publicized through newspapers, magazines, radio, television. There has been lively interest in Pennsylvania Dutch antiques and folk art and textile designs, and in Pennsylvania recipes. You can spend a "Pennsylvania Dutch Weekend" in the Amish country via a hotel bus-tour, or do similar sight-seeing by means of one-day group bus trips out of Philadelphia, Baltimore, or Washington. The Amish have been gawked at, puzzled over, envied, patronized, lionized. But somewhere along the way, their identity as individual human beings has become obscured.

9

Who Are the Amish?

If we are to bring them back in focus as people instead of dolls on a gift-shop shelf or stylized figures on wallpaper, it will be by watching them as they worship their God, play their games, plow their fields.

The Amish do not approve of photographs of themselves. It says in the Bible, "Thou shalt make no graven image," and a photograph is a graven image so far as the Amishman is concerned. That is why the photographs in this book are unique. They could have been obtained only in the way they actually were—by a photographer who has lived all his life in Amishland, known hundreds of Amish, used vast patience and guile and caution and understanding. The Amish chose to ignore his camera, did not see it—or were just not fast enough to dodge.

Some of the pictures have appeared in various publications, magazines and newspapers, notably the *Sunday News* in Lancaster, Pennsylvania. It was *Sunday News* Editor Tom Barber who shook his head over some of Charlie Rice's beautiful salon prints some years ago and pointed out what was wrong with them; since then, Rice prints have won no exhibition prizes, but each has told a story.

The photographs and words in this book are intended to tell something of the way the Amish of one community really live, to show what they might be doing at a given time during the year. Most writing about the Amish has been "sympathetic." In this book the authors have tried to keep clear of either sympathy or criticism, to stick to straight reporting, to avoid easy generalizations. What you read and see here concerns the Amish settlements of

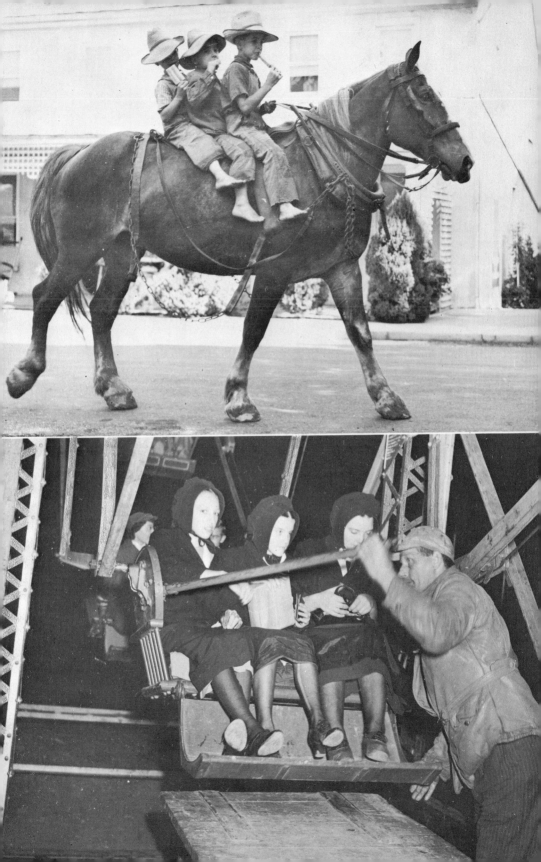

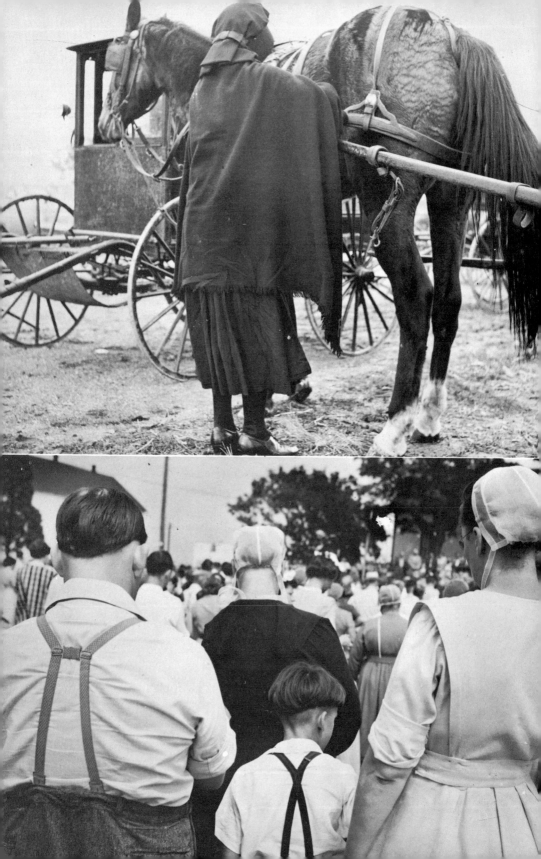

Lancaster County, Pennsylvania, the oldest, though not the largest, of the Amish communities in America. It does not follow that precisely these same things happen among the Amish of Ohio, Maryland, Indiana, and elsewhere in the nation, or, indeed, that they will happen in just this way again in Lancaster County. Our guess is, however, that the Amish will still be here, much as they are today, for generations to come.

Probably the most remarkable fact about these remarkable people is that they are maintaining their way of life although they are not insulated by a backwoods environment. Their farms border the Pennsylvania Turnpike, the Pennsylvania Railroad, the Lincoln Highway. They live next door to non-Amish, do business with them, ride with them on buses, walk with them on the streets of the city. Almost all Amish are farmers. With their physical strength and mechanical aptitude, they would be welcomed on the payrolls of such long-time Lancaster industries as Armstrong Cork and Hamilton Watch, or the newer RCA, Alcoa, and Schick plants. None of them work in these major industries, nor in the myriad smaller ones close by, but it's not for lack of intelligence.

They know all about radio and television, though they are not permitted to own receivers. One neighbor tells of catching a young Amishman on his porch, peering through the window at a late-evening TV show. When the porch light was turned on, he stammered that he had just come over to borrow a hatchet. Invited in, he stayed to see the show before leaving with the hatchet. A week later he returned the tool at the same hour, just in time for the opening commercial.

14

Lancastrians relish such stories about their Amish, much as other Americans enjoy local tales of the Crackers, the Ozark mountaineers, the back-country Mormons. Some of the Lancaster stories are apocryphal; others bear the stamp of fact. But all tell something about both the Amish and the non-Amish of Lancaster County.

For instance, there's the famous one about the Amishman who bid in a small farm at public sale for $40,000. He sent his wife home with instructions to dig up the bucket buried out back of the hog pen. She returned, the money was counted, but there was only $35,000. "Ach, Mom," exclaimed the Amishman, "you got the wrong bucket!"

Then there was the Amish huckster who brought his 12-year-old son along in the market wagon every Saturday morning when he called on his regular customers in Lancaster. One buyer complained that she'd found some bad apples in the quarter-peck the Amishman sold her the week before. "Why," said the Amishman, "I didn't hear nobody else complain," and, turning to his son, "Did you, Jonathan?" Jonathan answered, "Yah."

And there was, too, the young Amish mother who herded an uncomfortable-looking brood of youngsters into a Blue Ball general store and said to the clerk: "We chust come in to go out; where is it?" She was directed to the rest rooms.

These stories represent one attitude; there are others. Some Lancastrians are impatient with the Amish about one or another of their rejections of modernity. Some actively dislike them. Some glorify the Amish as models of

15

simplicity we would all be happier in emulating. Some coldly regard them as an economic asset. Some are simply fond of them for what they are and represent.

Neighbors of the Amish have, in the course of things, created and maintained many myths about them. The Amish have been known to tell some real whoppers about themselves. Much has been written about the blue gate that means a marriageable daughter, and the hex sign on the barn to ward off evil spirits. You can read elsewhere the statistics (16,731 Old Order Amish church members in the United States, according to the 1956 *Mennonite Year-book*); the funny-looking Dutch phrases (the late H. L. Mencken studied Pennsylvania Dutch for years before visiting Lancaster, and then was stunned to discover he couldn't understand a word of it); the scholarly studies by the experts (there are a number of entries under "Amish" in library indices and *Readers' Guide*—even the French had a chance to read in *Le Monde* an illuminating article entitled "De Turnpike à Intercourse; Week-End Chez les Amish"). We do not yet have the anthropological, biometric, and sociological studies which should be made of the Amish by trained observers; they are overdue.

What we describe in this book is true, to the best of our ability to portray it. In the process, some of the simplicity traditionally imputed to these people may be shown to have been exaggerated. We hope *The Amish Year* shows a community, not of cast-iron toy figures or Protestant plaster saints, but of very human beings, deeply involved in their beliefs and their family relationships, hard-working, yet as ready for fun and laughter as the rest of us.

19

JANUARY

"Sold to Jacob Lapp!"

The auctioneer breathed one foggy breath into the cold morning air, then asked, "Jake, what the dickens are you going to do with it?"

Jake grinned between the broad brim of his black hat and the black bristle of his chin-whiskers and said nothing. He handed the clerk $28.50 in slightly soiled currency. Half a dozen other bearded men, who looked remarkably like Jake at as many different ages, helped him lug the electric refrigerator to his open spring wagon and rope it upright. He stood for a moment admiring the thing, shining in the cold sunlight like a hog-tied iceberg, and then returned to the sound of selling.

Everybody in the crowd of about one hundred people around the auctioneer knew that Jacob Lapp had no electric power on his farm. If the Pennsylvania Power and Light Company were to string a wire to his back door today, there would be a delegation of Amish churchmen at his front door tomorrow. Nobody at the sale knew why Jake had bought a refrigerator, but everybody was certain that Jake knew what he was doing.

About half the people wandering around the Lancaster

County farm sale that day were fellow churchmen of Jake Lapp. It was not an Amish farm that was on the block, but it was on the edge of Amish country, and the land would be bid high. And there was always that delightful possibility of a good bargain among the house furnishings and the farm equipment that would all change hands before the clerks wrote out the last of the transactions around sundown.

There's a fairly accurate tradition in Lancaster County that an Amishman will buy land, but won't sell it. At least, the domain of the Amish always seems to be getting a little bigger, instead of shrinking in the fashion that might be expected of the holdings of a sect which by all the laws of evolution should have died out or conformed to the progressive ways of the world a century ago.

It might be supposed that economic competition would have eliminated any group which lives in the center of one of the nation's great concentrations of electric power but never uses a kilowatt of it. Ask an Amishman why he doesn't use electricity, and he'll probably answer with a shrug. If he's one of the talkative kind, he may say, "It's worldly." Actually it's an Old Order Amish church rule. But since there are no written church rules, this would be hard to prove. Let's just say that Jacob Lapp has known, ever since he was old enough to understand, that the Amish don't use electric power.

Jacob Lapp had no intention of buying this farm. But he knew pretty much who would. Moreover, his guess of $1,050 per acre for the 65-acre property was within a few dollars of what his friend Benuel Petersheim actually would pay for it later in the day.

There were off-gray patches on the knees of Jake's plain, gray pants, and his heavy, buttonless, gray jacket looked shabby. But he paid cash for everything he bought. So did all the other Amishmen there—including Benuel Petersheim when he counted out the price of the farm.

Jacob had walked through the house and glanced at the tables heaped up with kitchen and dining things, while Mrs. Lapp followed along and once or twice whispered to him about something she'd like him to buy. The two Lapp children, and a dozen other Amish youngsters, had been left discreetly outside, away from the perilously balanced china and glass.

An auction sale can be a sad thing, for it may mean death or bankruptcy or simply old age. In Lancaster County it's usually the last. You'd wait long for a sheriff's sale in the Amish country; these are money-making farms. The barns could hold four red New England barns, and there are tobacco sheds larger than a three-story house, chicken coops that look like small hotels, and vast old farmhouses designed to hold families of seventeen or eighteen without crowding.

At the sale where Jacob Lapp bought the electric refrigerator, things went as they do at hundreds of farm auctions every year in Lancaster County. People came early. There was still a fringe of frost on every piece of machinery strung out along the lane for easy inspection. A few of the older Amish wore heavy overcoats. Mostly, however, it was just pants and jackets for the men, shawls and skirts for the women. They padded out underneath to suit the weather.

26

A farm sale is a holiday for the Amish. For a really big one, the children are excused from school. No matter how rough the weather, most of the selling is done outdoors. Usually there's an improvised ring, where the animals are paraded before the bidding. Tools, machines, hay in the mow, corn in the crib, all are sold.

Winter is the best time for an auction, because field work is slack and there will be opportunity for the new owner to settle in before the spring planting. Especially after the Christmas holidays, the country printers' order books fill up with sale bills. The auction which made Jake Lapp the temporary owner of an electric refrigerator was advertised by such bills, printed on coarse paper 16 by 20 inches, headed in big block letters "FARM SALE." The farmer had three hundred printed and distributed them to stores for some miles around. Old handset type proclaimed the items to be sold, and the printer contributed, as an aesthetic touch, the woodcuts of a horse and a cow whose lines were somewhat smudged by fifty years under the ink roller.

It was no trickery that all the harness was greased and mended in the weeks before the sale, the manure-spreader carefully cleaned, the cattle groomed and curried at the final moment. Every piece of the equipment ranged along the lane had been painted bright orange or screaming red. No one supposed it to be new, but the price of the paint was more than made up in higher bids.

The auctioneer knew not only Jake Lapp, but practically everybody else in the crowd. He knew them by name and by reputation and used his knowledge like a

master swordsman. Beginning with the formal announce-
ment of the owner's name, he continued with the regular
warning. "All terms are cash, and all articles must be
moved off the premises within the week." He started with
small tools, always in demand, to sharpen up the bidding.
He crawled onto a wagon or a fence rail or any other spot
where he could watch for the raised finger, the nod or
wink, that meant a bid. His clerk stood close by with pad
and pencil. If bidding flagged, the auctioneer would prod
a fat farmer about how much weight he'd lost, or tell a
quick, barnyard-level joke in Dutch, or rap resoundingly
on an empty wagon bed with his cane, the badge of his
trade, to snap attention back to his spiel.

Jacob Lapp had no interest in the pile of a hundred
locust posts onto which the auctioneer had scrambled to
take bids, so he headed back to the wagon shed where
he'd earlier sniffed coffee steam. Here a couple of enter-
prising Amish girls, interested in enlarging their dowries,
had set up some rough boards used in the bottom of the
hay wagon during haymaking, and were doing a thriving
business in coffee from a huge, old, gray enamel pot, boiled
hot dogs, and fried hamburgers on buns, all prepared on
a smoky oilstove just behind the splintery counter. The
soft pretzels Jake had bought earlier from the huckster
circulating in the crowd hadn't been enough even to stir
up his appetite, so he splurged on thirty cents' worth of
hot dogs and coffee over the lunch counter. He wondered
why there wasn't some chicken corn soup, too. For dessert,
he bought a pint of ice cream. Just as he was opening the
end of the box, up came not only his two little boys, but

his wife as well. But he'd spent enough now. They could just help eat the pint of ice cream. They all sat perched on a cold pile of lumber, taking turns at the ice cream box. Around them a fine shower of blowing snow turned to silver and disappeared, as the sun popped out like a sudden spotlight on the barnyard.

All the while, the sale was progressing from tools to machines to livestock to furniture. There was a noticeable stir when the helper held up a wooden chair, and the auctioneer called, "How much am I bid for these fine old plank-bottom arrow-backs? There's six of them, all perfect—ain't they, Si?—and that looks like the original paint."

This was the cue for three or four antique dealers, who had been conscientiously avoiding one another all day, to move in for the kill. Sometimes a bunch of old kitchen chairs that nobody has thought much about for years will bring twenty and thirty dollars apiece.

Jacob and his ample wife waited patiently on the frost-humped front lawn as the utensils went on sale. A pair of iron skillets, black from the frying of untold tons of potatoes was passed through the window by a helper inside. The skillets were sold together, for 35 cents. Then came half a dozen matching cups, with five saucers (two nicked). These were succeeded by a soap carton filled with everything that had been in the kitchen cupboard drawer, from a cracked wooden potato masher to a bone-handled carving knife, stoned down to a sliver of steel.

The Lapps were waiting for the large and undistinguished serving dishes from the second-best shelves. Some

33

34

of theirs had been cracked and broken by overly helpful young girls of the congregation, the last time they'd entertained, and Mrs. Lapp knew just how many open bowls and how many covered dishes she should have to replace the breakage and what size they should be. She got most of what she wanted in a burst of bidding in which Jake carried off half a dozen pieces for five, ten, and fifteen cents each. The last one somebody else wanted more, and Jake quit at a quarter. There'd be another sale.

In Lancaster County, there will always be another sale. They happen all year 'round. Sometimes everything goes. Sometimes an Amish couple just decide to sell out a lot of their belongings and retire at fifty or so, to let the younger folks do the farming. For the larger sales, newspapers carry classified ads, often running to three or four columns of agate type at the height of the auction season. Good prices for land or personal property (it's not unusual for a locally made grandfather clock to go for over $500) are reported not only in the papers of the county towns, but also those of Lancaster City.

There are other kinds of sales to attract the Amishman, with his typically American love of a bargain. Several sales barns are operated in Lancaster County where all kinds of livestock are put on the block.

In an average year, there are more horses than automobiles sold in the county. In 1954, for example, 7,521 automobiles were sold in Lancaster County, but the New Holland Sales Stables alone sold 15,000 horses and mules. The secret of the popularity of the horse is twofold. In the first place, the Amish must have horses to run their

farms and to travel in the vicinity. In the second place, there is a tremendous market for the old and decrepit horse; no longer does he go to the glue factory, but to the dog-food industry. As a center of four-footed horsepower, Lancaster naturally became, as well, a center for the purchase of material for canned dog-food.

Such statistics, however, did not concern Jake Lapp, as he and his little family and his big refrigerator drove homeward in the late January afternoon. The blacktop road was still grayed in spots with snow blown into the surface roughness by the last flurry. The horse, happily homebound, snorted when Jake reined in beside the farmhouse of an "English" neighbor. Without turning his head, Jake spoke to his wife:

"I think I'll just stop in at Zimmerman's place once. His daughter's getting married next month." A pause while two autos overtook and passed them. "He said he'd give fifty dollars if he could find a good second-hand refrigerator for her."

FEBRUARY

"Noah, your mutzi is wore out."

Noah King had suspected this was coming; at last, his wife had said it. The mutzi, the black frock coat that he kept in the closet for churchgoing, would have to be replaced.

He'd bought it to be married in nine years ago. Now his wife's most expert needlework could no longer disguise the thin spots or the rips in the tired worsted. Furthermore, in bright sunlight the coat had a greenish look, as though some microscopic moss had sprouted between the stitches.

"You got nothing to do tomorrow. We'll go in to Lancaster. And I guess you better get a new pair of pants and a vest to go with."

Noah felt the vest was still pretty good, but he kept this to himself.

Next morning found the Kings on the second floor of the Hager and Bro. department store, just across the alley from Lancaster's Central Market where their neighbors sold dressed poultry Tuesdays and Fridays. They'd got a ride to the city in their friends' market wagon, arriving at 6:00 A.M., then had poked around the stalls until the store opened.

"Bigger," observed Noah's wife as they progressed among the dress-goods counters toward the discreetly enclosed Plain Clothing Department in the rear. It had been several years since they were here, and they could see that the department had extended its partition some distance into the main store.

Hager and Bro. is just one of a number of outlets for Plain clothing, which some people sell right from their homes. But the store has what is probably the world's largest department devoted to this merchandise. Here almost all the "lady clerks" wear the prayer coverings over their hair which mark them as members of one or another of the Plain Sects. Their customers belong to at least a dozen different denominations whose customs dictate the wearing of distinctively unadorned clothing.

These Plain Sects, most of which you can find represented in various parts of Lancaster County, include the strict River Brethren (the stock which produced Dwight D. Eisenhower), the Yoneyites and Amish Mennonites, and the more liberal Mennonites and Brethren. Some members of the latter two wear clothes in no way distinguishable from those of the majority of their fellow-Americans.

The Amish account for only about 10 per cent of her business, it is estimated by Mrs. Lillian Ebersole, the department manager, who's been at Hager's since 1936. This keen-eyed, motherly Mennonite has few worries about quick-changing styles, but she must keep alert to the slow trends in the sartorial preferences of her Plain friends.

Noah King knew the mutzi he'd buy here would be of exactly the same cut, stitch for stitch, as the hook-and-eye coat he had just discarded—the first store-bought garment of his lifetime. The same tailor, who's been on the job for some twenty years, would do the work. The broadfall trousers, too, would look the same. The vest would differ only in the matter of some slight expansion in waistline measure.

But Noah scratched his head over the fabrics. The herringbone looked nice, but so did the serge. His old wedding coat was black. Should he change to oxford gray, maybe, or the navy blue? The clerk showed him the bolt of gabardine from which some of the younger Amish had been ordering suits, but wasn't surprised when Noah gave it only a quick glance.

There's no special difficulty in getting the drab fabrics that Amishmen favor. Many of the largest mills supply them in pure wool worsteds. Hager's does not keep ready-made Amish suits on hand, except for a few demonstration models, which are used to show what the finished product will look like. Recently, one was bought off the rack by one of the numerous tourists who visit the store.

Amish never order extra pants, Mrs. Ebersole says, though they may go in for an extra jacket; the mutzi, frock-backed with long tails, will be bought for church, while a sack coat may be wanted for everyday use. Three or four sack coat models are available, the principal differences being in the neckband, which may be high or cut in a V (no lapels or pockets, in any case), and in the bottom front, where the corners may be cut curved or square. All close with hook and eye. Zippers are not used. Why? To

44

others they may look at least as inconspicuous as the hook and eye, but to the Amishman, they're new, modern, "worldly."

The broadfall trousers have no fly. They button along the top and down the sides, like a baby's overalls. These trousers, which also resemble sailor pants, are referred to as "barn-door britches." They are held up by wide suspenders, which are often homemade. Frequently work pants end high up the calf, which may look odd in town, but which makes sense for traveling down a furrow. High shoes are usually worn, but even in freezing weather an Amishman may appear on the city streets barefoot. He may be equally brash in coming to town unshod when the asphalt is egg-frying hot in summer. The non-Amish permit themselves to wonder occasionally if their Plain friends are not showing off, just a little, how tough their callused soles have become.

Noah could have ordered a three-piece outfit for less than $50, but he preferred the better fabrics and ended up paying $83.50. He might have gone even higher.

While her husband was musing over the narrow choice, Mrs. King was looking at the few items which she might buy here for herself. In the Plain Clothing Department, she would look for no ready-made dresses, for Amish women make all their own clothes, and their children's, too. She might admire the snowy, imported Swiss organdy used for prayer coverings, and possibly buy enough for a couple of extras for herself and her daughters, together with the tiny mesh frames on which the cloth is sewn. There was a choice of permanent-finish organdies, at $1.39 and $1.98 a yard. An unmarried Amish girl at the same

counter was looking at the domestic organdies—69 and 89 cents a yard—from which the Amish maidens make their pretty white aprons.

A few acceptable dress fabrics are sold here—lusterless blacks in Romaine crepe and spun rayon. Others are outside among the yard goods.

Mrs. King glanced at the sweaters, sized for men and women, and knit in oxford gray and black. They button down the front, but for some reason this is not offensive to the Amish, even though they insist on hook-and-eye closures for most other outer garments. The Amish also knit sweaters for themselves, sometimes making them extremely heavy for outdoor wear on such frosty days as this.

Neither Noah King nor his wife wore an overcoat, though the ride in the unheated market wagon had been bitter cold. It's mostly the older men who wear the long coats. This may be one of the rare changes of fashion among the Amish. Nowadays Noah and his brethren simply don another layer of clothes when the mercury falls.

There are buttons on the greatcoats, probably because experience proved no hook and eye could be made heavy enough to hold. Again, the Amish feel no apparent contradiction in insisting upon a hook-and-eye jacket under a buttoned overcoat.

Though Hager's doesn't keep a model of the cape-coat on the racks any more, another large dealer in Plain clothes, Rubison's, at New Holland, reports some demand for it.

The tailor at Rubison's has found that his Amish customers always want their suits fitted loosely. You'll never see an Amishman in a "sharpie" jacket. What you might observe in his clothing is a hard-to-identify similarity to something else. The overcoat with its cape around the shoulders, the suit-coat with its squared-off, stand-up collar—where have you seen their like? Of course, in those perennial movies of West Point. The cadet at the United States Military Academy wears a uniform tailored like the costume of the pacifist Amishman. Except that his jacket collar is a little less of a choker, Noah wears clothes almost identical with those of the army's élite. He's more likely to be a C.O. (conscientious objector) than a C.O. (commissioned officer) in wartime, however, though there have always been some Amish youths whose adventurous spirit drove them to enlist during national emergencies. The similarity in dress is due, not to any parallel in role or outlook, but to the fact that for cadet and Amishman, styles crystallized in the distant past— about a century and a half ago.

February is a good clothes-buying time. Duties on the farm are light, and if an early bidder has paid off on the tobacco in the barn there's ample ready cash. Just before the November wedding season there will be another spurt in the department, and still another just before Christmas. The gift items which are generally most popular are the black, clip-on bow ties. White elastic armbands are on sale here, too.

So are hats. Amishmen's hats may look all alike at first glance, but there are subtle differences. The older men favor the flat-top model with the plain brim. Brim widths

from 3⅛ to 3¾ inches may be found on the shelves. Younger fellows like a round-topped hat, telescoped— pushed down evenly all around, pork-pie style. They often pick rolled-brim models, too. All Amish felt hats are black, with narrow black bands. Prices are $8.95 and up. For summer, there are straw hats on similar lines.

While Noah was finishing his order, Mrs. King wandered out of the Plain Clothing Department and into Yard Goods, just outside. She might have been looking for the heavy blue denim or covert cloth from which she makes Noah's overalls, but she wasn't. Her eye had been caught by the rainbow of those special colors which the Amish love, and which set off their somber outer garments so startingly. For her own and her daughter's blouses and skirts, for her husband's and her son's shirts, there were bolts of dull-finish cotton fabrics in Kelly green, yellow, red, royal blue and soldier blue, purple and plum. Handsome rayon acetates and broadcloths in these shades, and in navy and black, too, were there to tempt her. Amish men don't ordinarily have more than a minimum of clothing, but the women sometimes own rather large wardrobes.

On another counter were wildly colorful calico prints. Mrs. King wouldn't be caught dead wearing such worldly stuff, but she'd buy quantities of it—bolts of it, in fact— to be sewn into quilts. For a very tiny daughter she might buy a fabric with a very tiny figure, but it's not often done.

Noah's wife was dressed for town, but only the quality of the goods set off her costume from what she would wear around the house. Under a candle-snuffer black bonnet,

which concealed every strand of her yellow hair, she wore another, hidden bonnet, the white organdie prayer covering, which she would keep on if the outdoor hat were removed. Her simple under-dress, which extended to within about eight inches of the floor, was the same gray as the paint on the King's family wagon. (She had dresses of many bright colors at home, hanging in the large room which she used as a clothes closet, but she preferred the somber hue for city wear.)

Over the voluminous skirt, she wore a black apron. Its wide belt caught at the rear the point of the black overgarment, much like a stole, which spread over her shoulders and formlessly down the front to disappear again beneath the belt of the apron. White-headed straight pins—five of them—secured the belt in the back. She had taken off the heavy gray shawl—fringed and coming to a point at the rear—which served her instead of a topcoat.

Prices have gone up for Amish clothing and goods, just as they have for other store items. The Amish never complain, Mrs. Ebersole says. The closest thing to a complaint would be the occasional reasonable request for alteration of something such as sleeve length.

It's always a straight cash deal, too. No Amishman ever asks for credit, says Mrs. Ebersole.

There is a large mail-order business in Plain clothing. Orders come to Hager's from other Amish settlements in Pennsylvania, including the new settlement in Lebanon County and the very old one in the Middle Valley around Bellville, and are especially heavy from the large Amish communities in Ohio, Illinois, and Indiana.

If there's any territorial difference, it would seem to evidence itself in greater conservatism on the part of the Lancaster County Amish, Mrs. Ebersole believes. For example, a Lancaster Amishman might be more likely to buy the mutzi for everyday wear as well as for church, while the less formal sack coat would be used for "run-around" wear in other communities. This varies with individual preference, but Lancaster conservatism in clothes is definite.

In the process of growing up, an Amish child goes through several stages of clothing styles. Baby gowns will be made by mother, grandmother, relatives, and friends. From about one to three years, the child will wear a woolen cloak, for all baby clothes are made of wool. As soon as it's ready to toddle, the youngster will start to wear a homemade miniature of the clothing of its elders. Tiny bonnets and severely plain dresses—in extravagantly brilliant colors—will adorn the girls. The boys will have long pants and straight jackets and little, round, flat hats.

All her life, the girl's clothes will be home-sewn. The boy won't get his first real store-bought suit until he's about 16 (or size 34). He might get a ready-made suit before that, but even if he did, it would be made for the store by a neighbor, a seamstress, instead of by an out-of-town tailor.

Quite possibly, an Amishman might start out for a wedding or a funeral wearing a complete outfit of which not a stitch was made at home. This would include a ready-made white dress shirt of the sort now popular among the Lancaster Amish. It is known commercially as

"white on white"—white broadcloth with a white rayon stripe.

Despite this, his everyday wear is likely to be predominantly the product of his wife's needle. He might not visit the clothing department of a store for several years at a stretch. But, as one tailor observed, "When they buy, they buy good."

On this snowy February day, Mrs. King was happy to spot a non-Amish neighbor shopping a few aisles away, and quickly arranged to ride home in the neighbor's car. She wouldn't own an automobile, but has no reluctance about riding in one. She bustled back to tell her husband, but he pleaded the necessity for a visit to the hardware store across the street (it's the oldest in the United States, incidentally) and promised to take the next bus home.

Enjoying the novelty of an hour's freedom in town, Noah walked around the Court House block and back again to the Civil War monument in Penn Square, nodding a polite hello as he went to a lot of people he thought maybe he knew. He ambled past the movie theaters, examining the bright posters. He sidled into a cigar store and bought himself three ten-centers, then examined the racks of paperback books. A glance at the clock showed he still had about half an hour till bus time, so he counted out 35 cents for a book, shoved it inside his coat, and headed for the bus stop. There he settled himself comfortably in the cold sunlight on a stone stoop, and pulled out the book. In a moment he was immersed in the story, only his black hat showing above, and his curly brown beard below, the shiny cover of *The Girl from Easy Street.*

MARCH

"Look at that poor old man following the horse and plow. I thought everybody had tractors these days." So said the lady in the Connecticut convertible, driving along the Old Philadelphia Pike.

Despite his flowing chin-whiskers and the patch on the seat of his pants, the man guiding the plowshare was neither old nor poor. He was Elam Stoltzfus, Amishman. Had the lady's car broken down at that moment, Elam—age 42, owner of 84 paid-off acres—would probably have been able to get it going again.

But Elam himself owns no automobile. The power to run this farm comes from horses and the feed he raises for them, from the wind spinning the windmill, from the brook whirling the little iron water wheel. From God, he'd say if you asked him. But Elam is somewhat of a mechanical wonderworker, as, indeed, are most Amishmen, as well as their non-Amish farmer neighbors in Lancaster County.

Elam could afford an auto, a tractor, a deep-well electric pump, mechanical milking machines, all the power equipment that science has dreamed up to make the farmer's life easier and his bank account smaller. Not to mention an electric washing machine, and all the other "necessities" for his wife. Amishmen, however, spurn the aid—and the expense—of vehicles energized by petroleum products or motors run by electricity.

Of course, Elam will ride in a car. He'll even offer earnestly to pay the driver as much as it would have cost to ride the same distance by bus. No more, though.

If the Connecticut lady had been truly observant, she'd have noted several things more important than the misleading pants-patch and whiskers. She would have seen that while Elam's plow was shearing through the damp brown loam on hilltop and lowland alike, the non-Amish farmer next door wasn't plowing at all. His pretty red tractor stood idle in the barn. For the tractor was too heavy for the soil on this warm and windy March morning. Where Elam's sleek mare leaned into the traces and left hoofprints two or three inches deep for the plow to turn under, a tractor would have bogged down.

Had the passerby stopped for a look inside the wagon shed and barn of the Stoltzfus farm, she'd have come away with more respect than pity for proprietor of this estate.

She might have swung open the ponderous, but well-balanced doors to the shed, whose roof leaned against the stone wall of the barn on one side and topped a screened-in corncrib on the other. There she would have seen a collection of wheeled vehicles such as she never knew existed outside an 1880 Sears, Roebuck catalogue.

Naturally there would be Elam's boxy, closed-in family wagon, and his teen-age son's bachelor buggy. And the open-bodied market wagon. And the hay-ladder. And the heavy-duty hauling wagon. And the manure-spreader.

And the harrow and discs and tobacco planter.

Being a man of ingenuity and thrift, Elam manages to use the same chassis for a number of wagon bodies, some of which he has built himself, others of which came from the carriage maker's shop. The hay-ladder, for instance, could be unbolted from the frame and replaced with the tobacco ladder or the slant-sided body which Elam favors for handling his beautiful yellow squash.

Hung high on one wall is the gracefully curved sleigh. Elam knows without studying Baer's Almanac how far the spring has advanced. "The onion snow didn't make yet, but that never lays long enough for sleighing anyways."

Some of the larger wagon bodies are kept on the upper floor of the bank barn (so called because it can be entered at the upper level by means of an inclined driveway, built on a bank of earth piled at the rear of the building). Here the hay-ladder will be driven right onto the barn floor a few months hence, with the first fragrant load of sun-dried grass. This hay-ladder is a great, big piece of nothing much. It has no bottom to speak of, no sides, no rear end, and nothing in front but an eight-foot, ladder-like frame. Yet on this wagon, Elam and his boys can stack a towering load of hay. It's all in the way it's loaded. Unloading is tricky, too. It's done here with a pulley, which hoists large wads of hay up to the man who has one of the hottest, dustiest jobs in the world—spreading the hay in the mow. While he's wielding the pitchfork up near the roof at a temperature around 120°, he has to keep remembering that a false step could slide him down the hay-hole,

to land in front of a surprised cow some forty feet below, and quite possibly to crack his neck.

But in March, haying time is far enough away so that there remains a generous quantity of last year's crop in the barn. Beyond the organ-pipe noise of the wind in the pigeon-loft high above, and the stomp and murmur of the cattle below, there sounds a steady squeak-squeak-squeak which means that Elam's windmill is pumping water into the big iron trough along one side of the barnyard. Windmills always seem to squeak. This one, to avoid barnyard drainage, stands somewhat higher than the barn, on the very spot where Elam's friend, Simon Fisher, the Amish water-smeller, said there would be water. So strong was the pull of the hidden spring that it jerked the pliers right out of Simon's hands, though Elam could see he was hanging onto them so hard the sweat stood out on the backs of his strong fingers. (Simon Fisher long since discarded the willow twig used by old-fashioned dowsers. He found a good pair of pliers just as trustworthy, and always handy, so he didn't have to go cut a fresh fork down by the creek every time he was called on to find water.)

Most farms have three or four or more wells. One may fail or become contaminated, but even the worst drought seldom dries up all of an Amish farmer's sources of water.

The water with which Elam washes his hands and face and slakes his thirst at meals is pumped not by wind, but by water power. Fully three hundred yards from the house and over a small hill, so that it's not visible from the porch where Elam's washbasin hangs, is the lively little spring-fed stream which lifts pure drinking water from the old hand-dug well in the yard. Elam built a four-foot

dam at a likely spot in the brook and rigged up an over-shot water wheel just below it. The wheel, only about three feet in diameter, has a crank-like handle on one side. This bar is connected with another arm above, which is a seesaw, with a couple of large rocks wired on as counter-balances. The whole Rube Goldberg device is hitched to a wire which runs through ringbolts attached to short poles stuck in the ground, all the way to the house. And at the well, the turning of the water wheel and the rock-ing of the arm and the push-pull of the wire are converted into the up-and-down of a pump handle. And Elam Stoltzfus can wash his face. .

If you ask him what difference there is in principle be-tween his power device and the big hydroelectric develop-ments at Safe Harbor and Holtwood and Conowingo on the nearby Susquehanna, he probably would be hard put to it to explain. But he does know that the large alumi-num mailbox at the end of his lane will not contain any utilities bills at the end of the month.

Elam can't see much reason why he should stay up later than the chickens. He has to get up the same time they do, so why shouldn't he go to roost on their schedule? He'd use very little electricity for lighting even if he had the place wired. But being an Amishman, he uses kero-sene, which he calls coal oil. He buys it by the five-gallon can, usually plugging up the spout with a small potato. Now in March he won't be using so much, since the days are longer. About 8:00, though, you might see the soft light, as yellow as the butter Mrs. Stoltzfus churns, glow-ing in the kitchen window while Elam scans his newspaper.

69

Like many another farmer, Elam is always in the market for some outside work to supplement his income. There's a contractor "out back of Intercourse" who knows he can count on Elam to help dig a cellar any time except during the busiest farm seasons.

For Elam, despite his apparent rejection of modernity, is as expert a hand with a tractor and scoop as any man in the county. His trained team of bays responds no more readily to his command than the machine to his control. When there's a new house to begin, the contractor would rather have Elam backing out of the excavation than anybody else.

This activity of Elam's is accepted without censure by the elders of the church. But he has never even considered buying a tractor to do his own farm work.

Another of the little inconsistencies about Elam's way of life which outsiders find hard to explain is the ancient gasoline engine he uses for many odd jobs around the farm. The little one-lunger, bolted to a wheeled frame not much bigger than a child's coaster wagon, can be hitched by belt to a corn-sheller or silage-chopper or any of a number of other machines.

It emits a noise which many members of the younger generation have never heard, but which older folks know well. It is the offbeat, syncopated chug—chug chug—uh— chug of the one-cylinder gasoline engine which performed so many tasks on farm and homestead before it was displaced by the smoother-running, quieter electric motor thirty or forty years ago.

Perhaps the Amish have accepted the one-cylinder gasoline power plant just because it's been rejected by others as old-fashioned. Basically, it represents the same source of energy, the same mechanical process, which Elam finds too worldly when it's under the hood of an automobile.

There is, however, one thing about Elam's family that would bring the bishop up the front walk at a trot if he knew. But he doesn't. Neither, for that matter, does Elam. The truth is that Elam's son, Gideon, owns and drives a car.

Scrawny, skinny, beardless Gideon slips away in his bachelor buggy as often as he can and urges the horse down the highway to a commercial garage, five miles away. There, back in a corner, is the 1939 Ford he bought with his share of last year's tobacco money. For Gideon is a hot-rodder. He has rebuilt and tuned the engine, leaded and faired the body. Leaving the horse hobbled behind a nearby country schoolhouse, Gideon is off (and his wide-brimmed hat comes off, too!) to an old stretch of highway safely outside the Amish enclave for a prearranged drag race. Gideon's car was one of 26 driven by young Amishmen one year to the classic Whitmonday baseball game between the single and the young married Amish near New Holland.

Furthermore, if you glanced inside the boot of his buggy, you'd find his camera, a portable radio, a pair of slip-on oxfords (Amish are supposed to wear shoes which require some work to put on—either lacing or buttoning), the "English" cap under which he tucks his long hair when he's temporarily abandoning his Amishness (all non-Amish garb is "English"), and sometimes the wrist watch he is forbidden to wear.

March

When Father Elam steps down off the builder's tractor and returns to his horses, he seems content with his traditional lot. But will his son, Gideon, when he reaches the age of marrying and settling down, be satisfied to sell his beloved "rod" and bow out of the twentieth century?

Gideon can keep his car by quitting the Amish and joining the Mennonites. There is a special sect of ex-Amish calling themselves the Amish Mennonites, and these people have no rules against automobile ownership. Even if Gideon does backslide from the church of his fathers, it's probable that the rest of the Stoltzfus children will remain in the fold. And if only one in a family of six or seven pulls out, the Amish church is going to gain in membership—as, indeed, it has been doing at an impressive rate.

Probably, however, Gideon will do as so many young Amish have done in the past. He will join the church and quit shaving, get married, leave behind all the worldly enthusiasms of his youth, and be a good Amishman for the rest of his many days. For it should be remembered that the young folks who sometimes behave in what seems to be a very un-Amish way actually are not yet members of the Amish church. Around their families they follow the rules. Elsewhere they may not honestly feel bound to do so. They have the chance to decide for themselves as adults whether they will take the once-every-two-years opportunity of joining the church. Once they do, teen-age wildness is left behind for good.

APRIL

On this breeze-cooled April evening, Ammon Esh is wearing long underwear and a clean white shirt. No pants. For Ammon is dead, and the lower half of his coffin lid has been screwed on tight. It would be a waste to bury a good pair of trousers, and a shame to put a shabby pair on a corpse, and besides he is decently covered from the waist down.

The house is filled with Amish, plus a scattering of non-Amish folk who were Ammon's friends. They come in small groups to the almost bare room in which the body lies. On small tables, two chimney lamps burn steadily. Their yellow light catches glints in the beards— in varying shades of black, red, and gray—of the six quiet Amishmen who sit on straight-backed chairs around the body of Ammon Esh.

The unpainted box is of the classic coffin shape, as Amish carpenters have been fashioning them for generations—wider at the middle than at the squared-off ends. It rests on a pair of wooden sawhorses.

A girl cousin, her wide eyes filled with tears, leans over

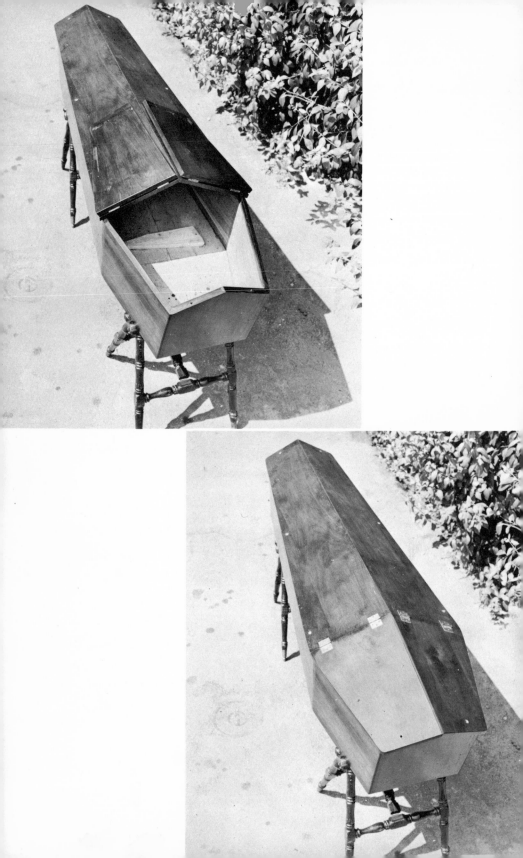

to look at the bearded corpse, lying in the plain white-pine box with its lining of simple white cotton cloth. Relatives, friends, neighbors, members of the congregation, bring their silent tribute to the dead. No flowers. There are never flowers at an Amish funeral.

As the hours pass, the stream of people moving through the room thins to a trickle. Finally it stops altogether. The house is silent and empty except for the family, now gone to bed, and the six men who keep the wake, and the corpse.

Do they pray? Do they whisper sometimes during the night, discussing the accident which cut off this big man in his prime? All of them were at the barn-raising when he slipped from a beam and fell twelve feet to the plank floor, and did not move again.

However they pass the night, they are still there at dawn, when the household begins to stir and prepare for the difficult day of the funeral. Many of the women relatives have had little time to mourn these past two days, for theirs is the responsibility of providing a luncheon which will be not unworthy of the dead man's reputation.

This is a big house, but by the time set for the funeral— 9:30 in the morning—it is shown to be far too small to hold the crowd. Nine hundred people, at a close guess, are swarming about the house and overflowing into the orchard and the lanes.

It is decided to move the funeral half a mile up the road to a huge red barn. Willing helpers quickly range scores of backless benches across the broad barn floor. Somber black, accented by the vivid shades of red and green and blue favored by the Amish for shirts and under-skirts and blouses, fills the dusty nave of the barn. Young-sters clamber up on the rafters and into the redolent hay-mow.

Ammon Esh, still in the half-closed coffin, is laid on the "bridge" of the barn—that is, the broad earthen ap-proach to the tremendous double barn doors, which have been swung open as far as they will go. This is a rural theater, with the audience inside the shadowed auditorium of the barn and the chief actor in the center of the brightly sunlit stage.

Services start at 10:00. The sun moves slowly up the morning sky as a wiry little man, with a wispy white beard straggling nearly to his waist, begins to preach.

In tones familiar to anyone who has ever been to a country church, the preacher quotes endlessly from Scrip-ture, in Pennsylvania Dutch. His oration rolls on and on, up and down, like the Amish hillside fields rolling to the horizon. Finally he says his amen and gives place to an-other speaker. And still another follows.

For two and a half hours, the solemn words pour steadily over the corpse and the silent mourners. At last it is over, and the people rise from the benches, the youngsters scramble down from the rafters and out of the hay, to pass once again around the coffin.

Some start for their buggies and home. But most return to Ammon Esh's house for the funeral dinner. By ten minutes to one, the first hundred have been seated at the outdoor tables. This is a huge crowd, so there will be only cold meats, some cooked vegetables, various kinds of

pickles, and dessert. At smaller funerals, there would be a hot meat dish as well—probably fried ham.

The women move swiftly to serve the first table. Plates bearing cold roast beef, sliced cheese, and cooked peas are set before each diner. Water glasses are filled. Family-style platters of pickled red beets, hard-boiled eggs, and several kinds of relish fill the centers of the tables. As soon as the first group has cleaned up its pie and cake, the people move away from the tables to make room for others.

Though some six hundred will be fed this way, those who wait are so quiet—even the tiny children—that the whining of the tires of a big truck on the highway a mile away sounds as plainly as a mosquito's hum at your ear.

So it goes until the last table is served, sometime after 3:00 in the afternoon. Plates are hastily rinsed between servings. Tumblers are just refilled. By the time the last table is seated, there are smears of beet juice and egg yolk spattered generously across the once-white cloths. Many of the glasses have cookie crumbs in them from the dunkers who went before. Nobody appears to mind.

At last it is finished. The exhausted women who cooked and served turn from cleaning up to pay their last respects to the dead. By 3:45 the men are hitching up the teams again. One horse is hitched to the hearse, which looks much like an ordinary Amish market wagon except that it is slightly larger and its sides are solid instead of being of canvas. A brother of the deceased climbs onto the seat and picks up the reins. It takes a long time for the funeral procession to form, but at last the hearse moves slowly

out onto the blacktop road, and the rest of the buggies follow, just about a carriage-length apart. There are nearly two hundred in the moving line.

This is a typical Amish funeral. Sometimes a more ornate hearse is used, one of those kept specially for the Plain trade by New Holland undertakers. Again, there may be some unorthodox detail, such as the white bow tie which Ike Huyard wore in his coffin. There were a thousand people at Ike's funeral, for he was well known and liked, by the non-Amish as well as the Amish.

It's six miles from Ammon Esh's house to his last resting place, and the buggies travel only about six miles an hour. There is time to think or to talk, as the buggy wheels squeak and crunch along side road and highway and finally through the quiet dust of the lane which leads to the Amish cemetery. The graveyard is surrounded by peaceful fields, where corn and tobacco and wheat and hay follow the rotation of the crops. The roofs of little Gordonville may be seen far down the road. Old trees grow at random in and around the hundreds of very simple headstones. There is a well-kept plank fence around all four sides. Several family plots are enclosed by iron pickets.

Since the moment when the non-Amish undertaker prepared Ammon Esh's body as the Pennsylvania law requires, he has been in the hands of those who knew and loved him. They watched by his side, they lifted him into the hearse. Now they gently lower the coffin to the turf, near the hole which has been dug by a kinsman.

There is no chaste little tent over the grave site. No

mats of plastic grass are laid to hide the raw, yellow clay. No dignified rail of chrome surrounds the burial place and awaits the touch of an undertaker's foot to start green tapes unreeling. There is no rough-box to give the illusion that this body will be sheltered from earth's everlasting chemistry that turns all to decent dust. There is no black-gloved mortician's assistant waiting for the family to depart before he finishes lowering the casket, gathers up the mechanical gadgets, and beckons for the hired diggers to come and finish the job.

Ammon Esh's own kin twist the screwdriver which fastens down the top half of the coffin, at last shielding his dead face from the sun; they let the pine box down into the hole; they take shovels and finish their task, from the first hollow rattle of clods to the final small heap of dirt, which in time will settle to the level of the rest of the graveyard.

Later a small, unadorned stone will be placed at Ammon's head—again by a close relative—and his family will have done all that's humanly possible for the body from which the soul has fled.

This day has seen a ceremony of rare dignity.

MAY

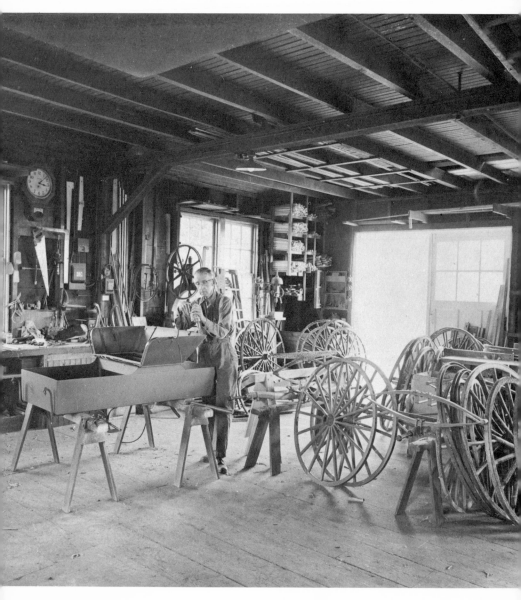

Harry Moore looked up from his work as the glistening new car swept past the wide-open doors of his shop. He caught a glimpse of the thin-faced girl at the wheel. The short, white ribbon dangling behind each ear from the prayer covering beneath her snug black Mennonite bonnet fluttered in the draft from the car window in the moment he could see her clearly.

Peering through his bifocals at the bearded man beside him, Harry Moore asked, "How soon are you Amish going to start driving automobiles and put me out of business?"

The Amishman pulled the raveled remainder of a home-rolled cigar from his lips and answered slowly, "Well, Horry"—he made it rhyme with "sorry"—"I guess when you get rich and retire, some young feller will be making buggies, still."

Harry Moore, carriage maker of Ronks, Pennsylvania, wasn't so sure. He knew no young fellows interested in learning his business. He had made a living at it for well over fifty years, but he knew even better than the boys at the trade school just how precarious its present status was. Harry is no Amishman, but he builds carriages for some hundred Amish families in the neighborhood of the village of Ronks, which stands along the main New York-to-Chicago line of the Pennsylvania Railroad and close to the Lincoln Highway.

"That girl's father paid around five thousand dollars for that car, Jesse," Harry Moore said. "He traded in an old model for part of the money—a two-year-old model, it was. How much are you paying for this wagon, if I ever get it done? And how long will you drive it?"

"You charge $560," Jesse answered readily. "I guess she ought to last me twenty, thirty years. Maybe all my life, if the Lord be willing."

Harry Moore thought of the private railroad crossing Jesse would have to negotiate near his farm, of the terrible speed of the streamlined diesels and the almost silent electric locomotives. He thought of the triple-lane highway, with trucks gunning for the foot of the Gap Hill and the constant rip-tide of traffic, and of Jesse sitting beside the stop sign on the open seat of his bachelor buggy (which his married state had made inappropriate for his use), waiting as much as five or ten minutes for the opening he needed. Harry hoped he'd still have a live customer when the job was done in about two weeks.

This family wagon for Jesse was one of the farthest advanced of several carriages a-building in the Moore shop. When Jesse was safely out of sight, Harry Moore turned away from the upended wooden box of the wagon body, to which he had been bolting a steel underframe. He stepped to the forge, where a long bar rested in the black coals, switched on the blower that started red

sparks hopping, and soon had the iron glowing. Practiced hands gripped the tongs, which withdrew the iron and slid it onto the anvil. The heavy hammer drew pyrotechnic sparks as it fell again and again, stroking the metal to the classic curve of a buggy axle.

Harry can still buy castings for axles. But he must shape them himself to just the right overhang and gather. (Proper overhang slants the front wheels so they are just two inches wider apart at the top than at the bottom. Correct gather toes them in precisely one quarter of an inch at the front, so they won't skid on crowned roads.)

Wheels from Hooper Bros. and Darlington of West Chester, Pennsylvania, are among the parts Moore can still buy ready-made. Axles come in two pieces and must be welded together as well as shaped. Moore must turn and cut the wooden hubcaps himself.

His wiry muscles tensed as he slung one of the wooden wheels onto an oaken wheelbuck he'd built as an apprentice. That was in 1899, at Dosch's shop in nearby Cambridge. An iron lever wrench he had hammered out that same year tightened the blocks to hold the wheel horizontally rigid. An electric drill holed through the wooden rim, and soon the iron tire was in place and bolted fast, completely blowout-proof and good for more years—if less mileage—than the finest rubber tire ever made in Akron.

A trio of Amish children, headed home, stopped by the door of the shop, fascinated by the orderly racks of tools and lumber, the unfamiliar hum of electric motors and the slap of endless belts, the smell of fresh shavings and of sprayed paint—all the paint being black or gray.

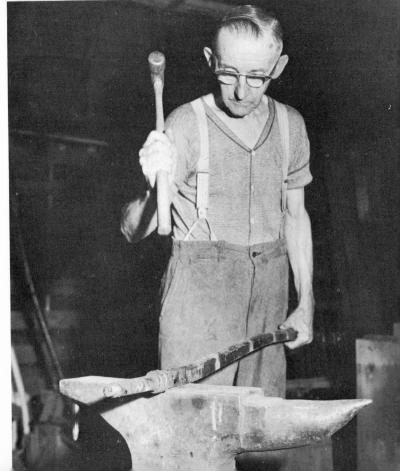

Goggle-eyed, they watched as the carriage maker meas- 'ured off a length of soft, green cloth from a fat bolt of material, chalked it, scissored it, laid it across the flaring seat back of an open buggy, where cotton batting was already tacked in place and trimmed. Methodically his tack-hammer moved along the frame, stretching on the covering with never a wrinkle. The children stared silently.

Out of an almost-flat face, completely surrounded by the sky-blue of a cotton bonnet, gray eyes looked with covert admiration at the heavy-duty sewing machine. Brown eyes, shaded by a broadbrimmed black hat, looked from an almost-round face toward the shiny half-horse motor, whose like would never be seen on the home farm.

In one corner of the shop was a board already sawed to seat-back shape, with coil springs nailed on and ready to be tied down to just the right tension. There was a plentiful supply of cotton batting and some more of the 70 per cent wool covering which would convert the seat back into a thing of comfort for tired backs jouncing over rutted roads.

Harry Moore likes to talk about his apprenticeship— three and a half years for a total wage of $100 including his room and board. But he talks, too, about the troubles of business today, which were unheard of when he opened his own first carriage shop at Blue Ball in 1903.

There was then no thought of a shortage of wagon-making materials. Today, some parts cannot be obtained at all and must be made. Others are to be had only in small quantities. Manufacturers from whom Moore buys such hardware as the round buggy steps, wheel stops, and

other castings tell him their dies are wearing out, and there's not enough business to make it worthwhile to replace them. Perhaps some new supplier will be found. If so, prices will be higher.

Harry makes both bachelor buggies and family wagons. The former, which are smaller, are priced at $420 complete, the latter at $560. That price covers a great lot of cutting, hammering, bolting, forging, fitting, painting. Each vehicle has the modern touch of dry-cell batteries under the seat, wired to lamps mounted on each side as prescribed by Pennsylvania law. Glass reflectors are mounted on the rear, as well. There's no shortage of these, at least, nor of the rear-view mirrors with which each wagon is supplied. Another safety device is the hand-operated brake assembly that clamps an iron block to the buggy tire, though a firm hand on the reins works faster in an emergency.

Elliptical springs on each axle make for an easy ride in a Moore buggy. There's the unseen but important fifth wheel, too. Anything but the drone its name has come to imply, this gear assembly at the pivot of the front axle permits the wheels to turn without upsetting the carriage. The rear wheels are bolted tight to the body spring, but the front spring is fastened to the top of the fifth wheel to which the front axle is attached below, allowing the front wheels a free swing on curves.

An auto's trunk has its counterpart in the buggy's boot. Here, just behind the seat, the heavy, waterproof lid protects spare harness, blankets, and sometimes groceries.

Before the fenderless buggy goes on the road, it is

equipped with some protection against the dirt from the road—a loosely hung sheet of leather between front axle and singletree at the point where flying hoofs will toss most mud.

Bachelor buggies have no roofs, but the more sedate family wagons have sides, back, and top of white cotton duck, painted gray with many coats of Harry's own special mix of oil paint. One wagon requires 7½ yards of this material. The rear curtain can be rolled up to let air through and to give the youngsters a wide rear view— offering a view even more fascinating, to those in a following automobile, of giggling or solemn faces under square-bobbed, blond hair, of the solid backs of father and mother outlined against the road ahead, and just the horse's ears and a whisk of tail to disclose the motive-power.

There's also a roll-up on each side of the front seat. It's kept up, generally, except in the coldest weather. Some Amish wagons have glass window screens for cold-weather use; some don't. Some also have sliding, windowed doors.

Harry Moore's finished product is a pretty sight. The spick-and-span gray of top and body contrast cleanly with the glossy black of the undercarriage, and in the structure there is a feeling of lightness and strength and calculated simplicity.

Moore is one of three or four active carriage makers in the Amish country around Lancaster. There are other artisans who repair vehicles for the Amish and, of course, the blacksmiths who keep the horses safely shod. Most of the blacksmiths have given up their smoky shops and

travel around the countryside with forges and anvils set up on truck bodies.

In his long half-century of craftsmanship, Harry Moore has built hundreds of carriages. Many have lasted the lifetimes of their owners.

"Funny thing, though, no Amishman has ever told me what a good job I did for him," Moore reflects. "On the other hand, not a one has ever complained, either."

It is quite possible that within a decade or two, a lack of coachmakers and carriage parts will force the Amish to accept ownership of automobiles, as the almost equally conservative River Brethren of some Lancaster congregations have done. The Amish are eminently practical people.

JUNE

The barn-raising is one of those pioneer traditions dear to America. The Amish have preserved it, as they have other customs, because it serves them well and is a lot of fun. A barn-raising among the Amish is a holiday from home, and though the work may be harder than the home chores, there's the zest of horseplay that most community gatherings of the Plain folk must lack. They may eat as heartily after Sunday services, at a wedding, and even at a funeral. But a barn-raising has no religious overtones to command restraint.

Perhaps it was the same way two hundred years ago when the folks got together to restore the neighbor's barn that had been burned by a disgruntled Indian. Call it animal spirits, primitive humor—things sometimes get a bit rough at an Amish barn-raising.

Yet, ideally, a barn-raising is a poem and a ballet. It represents communal effort at a high level of unselfishness. It proves the power of the organized crowd. It has a swing and a dash and a rhythm.

Christian Zook had an old tobacco barn which made

a midnight torch during the last thunderstorm. "Gusts" is what such storms are disarmingly called in Lancaster County. But don't be misled. A Pennsylvania thunder-gust can be a vicious thing.

Christian carried no insurance. An Amishman's neigh-bors are his insurance company. They pitched in to help fight the fire and then to help clear away the charred debris.

Chris was on his own for a few weeks between the time of the fire and the day of the barn-raising. He called in Henry Horning of Goodville, a respected boss carpen-ter, and together they figured how much and what kind of lumber and nails and hardware to buy. This is to be a 30 by 40 tobacco shed—not so big for Amish country, where the barns are just about the biggest in the world.

Horning and his men got the lumber cut to the right lengths and placed in handy piles. With hatchet and chisel the ends of the timbers were shaped for mortising and pegging. Meanwhile, the concrete-block crew laid the new foundation, in which there will be a tobacco cellar and stripping room where the whole family will spend long evening hours next winter, preparing the crop for the buyers.

Now the great day has dawned at last—or almost dawned. Friends and neighbors who must drive ten or fifteen miles to help at the big affair are getting up even longer before sunrise than usual. Livestock must be cared for and a hefty breakfast cooked and eaten and the home place left looking nice. The family piles into the buggy. Father switches on the battery-powered side lights. By the time they reach Zook's, lights are no longer needed.

Perhaps forty women were here yesterday to start the cooking. Today they will finish the business of stewing chickens by the dozen, frying potato chips by the bushel, mixing lemonade by the gallon.

Through the chill mist of the summer morning the buggies appear, coming by every road. An old bus weaves its way through the lightening fog to bring a load of "neighbors" who decided that the twenty or so miles from Chester County was just too far to depend on the horse. A few others have hitched auto rides with non-Amish families.

It's 7:00, and everybody's here that's coming. There are more than eighty men, most of whom have brought their own tools. A few turn up dressed for town, and take some rough kidding about fellows who come to a barn-raising just for the eats. There are always some who do; the crowd will have swelled to several hundred by lunch-time.

This tobacco shed will be a heavy-timbered structure. It must be built to hold hundreds of laths strung with to-bacco for drying. The framework is put together without nails, because it will last longer that way. Pegs are ham-mered home and mortises fitted neatly, as the first long oaken stringer is prepared for raising into place. Carrying-poles—short, strong wooden rods, rounded at both ends for firm handholds—are placed under the heavy beam, and a dozen men rise in unison to hoist it and carry it onto the temporary flooring laid as a working surface upon the new foundation.

Soon it is joined to two other timbers, the uprights of the first span. Long ropes are knotted around it. Sixteen men, with one unanimous grunt, raise it slowly. When it's at arm's length overhead, another gang moves in with iron-tipped pike poles to shove it the rest of the way up, and others hold hard to the ropes at the final moment to keep the whole span from going on over and down again.

As soon as there's a post to shinny up, the old men vie with the younger ones to see who will be the first up to a strategic position to guide in and pin fast the next important structural member. A sixty-year-old preacher tightropes along a beam like a steel-rigger. Whether it's because of the human urge to show off or an eagerness to do the job well, Amishmen are often injured, and some have been killed, at barn-raisings. Today, there's nothing worse than a few mashed thumbs and some long white-pine splinters, the latter removed expeditiously with the aid of the host's pocketknife.

There is little bossing. Occasionally the owner of the farm, who has stepped in to take his rightful place as foreman of the job, despite the presence of the boss carpenter, will shout for somebody he needs for a special task.

Since there may be eight or ten men there with the same name, he'll distinguish them by prefacing the call with the man's hometown. So it's "Elverson Jonas Lapp" here and "Monterey Sammy Fisher" there. (There are only about a dozen family names among the Amish in Lancaster County, due to vigorous inbreeding, and first names are likely to be drawn from the Bible, with many duplications.)

It's time for the first break. At home this would be the "ten o'clock piece," brought out to the field in a towel-covered basket by wife or daughter. Here at Christian Zook's barn-raising, appetites soar with the framework, and by 9:30 the girls are scurrying out with sandwiches and lemonade and doughnuts. The men have been working hard; they eat the same way, though this is just the appetizer for lunch at noon.

Astonishingly soon, a grinning graybeard is astride the rooftree or "purline," 26 feet above the rough flooring. He leans out perilously far and saws the mortised tenon, and this squared-off oak tree is in place for the next century unless another stroke of lightning intervenes.

By noon the galvanized roof is being nailed in place with the lead-headed nails which close up their own nail-holes.

There's a big barn door leaning against a shed nearby. One young Amishman, quitting a little early so he won't be late at table, looks cautiously around, then deposits his shiny new hatchet behind the door. Others do likewise. By the time dinner is served, the grass back there looks like a hardware store.

On an ugly day dinner might be served inside the big farmhouse. But this is a beautiful day. The fog has burned off, and the sun is hot on the shiny iron roof. The meal is a triumph for the women, who serve it on long tables made of planks on sawbucks and spread with white table-cloths, all in the shade of a generous sycamore tree. There is enormous enjoyment of an enormous quantity of food.

Afterwards, there is still plenty of work as the siding is

nailed in place. The corncrib along one entire wall of the barn takes shape. Hammers still rattle and saws whine. But the noise of the tools is gradually giving place to the sound of voices. Some of the men are running out of constructive things to do.

A stranger stops by to talk to one of the old men on the ground. As they stand close together to converse against the racket of fifty hammers pounding spikes and twenty saws trimming boards, a hammer suddenly falls from a high beam. With a thud, it lands in the middle of the crown of the old Amishman's black hat. A wisp of dust rises in the still air. The hammer falls to the ground. The old man never misses a word of his dialogue, doesn't look up. The stranger, however, becomes increasingly uneasy. He finds little more to say before he goes away almost at a trot, muttering. The old man then slowly removes his hat, scratches his head through a disordered mop of hair that must be at least as good insulation as a felt mattress, and goes on about his business.

It's a happy time for the youngsters. The prolific Amish bring the little ones along to have fun, and the older children to help. Tiny boys who might have posed for Renaissance angels sit by quietly and learn what happens at a barn-raising. There'll always be another generation that knows how to raise a purline—or nail a friend's claw-hammer to the floor while he isn't looking.

By about 4:00, everything's finished that is going to be. The barn looks pretty complete, though there is still much work to be done by carpenter Horning and his boys. By the time they've packed their tools and said good-by,

farmer Zook will have spent about $5,000. Probably several thousand dollars were saved for him by this one day's work. He will repay it by helping his neighbors as they have helped him.

Chris may pack up his hatchet and wood-chisel for traveling two or three times a year, for all Amish barns are built this way. During the World War II days of building-material shortages, gangs of Amish organized to buy and dismantle old barns on disused farms as much as a hundred miles away from their home communities. They would salvage every useable item and save it for a time of barn-raising need. There is still a highly efficient, all-Amish house-wrecking crew, which can often be spotted in the heart of Lancaster City, tearing down old buildings to make way for parking lots or new construction. They work for wages, of course, and are among the few Amishmen who aren't full-time farmers. At that, most of the wreckers live on farms and do some farming on the side.

But the Amish who waved a magic wand over Chris Zook's stacks of lumber this day and caused a tobacco barn to appear, were summoned by the savory smell of stewing chickens, the thought of walking the highest beam, the compulsion of centuries of custom.

The bachelor buggies and the market wagons start to stream away from the Zook farm while the sun is still well up the sky, for everybody goes home for supper. Cows must be milked, chickens fed. The reddening sky gilds the rolled-up rear flap of one of the gray wagons, in which five-year-old Aaron Hostetler is riding with his six-year-

June

old sister and his seven-year-old brother, with father and
mother on the front seat, and the brisk-footed brown
mare trotting happily homeward. Aaron is silent and a
little sleepy, but he is thinking of the day when he will
go to a barn-raising and tell the story of how Blue Ball
Benjamin Blank stole the new hat of Bareville Benjamin
Blank and nailed it good and hard to the highest rafter.
It's been a lovely day.

JULY

Cleon Yoder sat stolidly on the bare, board seat of his tobacco wagon and stared straight ahead over the rain-streaming backs of his matched gray mules. His square face with its straggle of young beard was the only dry part of the man, for it was protected by a broad hatbrim. The midsummer thundershower had blackened Cleon's gray shirt and plastered it against his back. His powerful hands gripped the slippery reins, and his rolled-up sleeves stretched taut over bulging muscles.

The off-mule shied, breaking step, as lightning lent each separate raindrop a moment's luminosity. Out of the murk ahead appeared a completely black sedan, swimming like a water beetle through the foot-high mist of bouncing rain. Cleon Yoder noted first that every bit of chrome on the car had been painted black—bumpers, grill, radiator ornament, headlight rims, and all. Then he peered through the arc of windshield cleared by the leaping wiper and saw a broad, bearded face under a wide, black hat. A hand waved as the car splashed by Cleon's rig. He nodded stiffly, and rain which had gathered in the pushed-down top of his own black hat cascaded past his face. Cleon drove on.

Half a mile farther, he geed the mules into a long lane. By now the storm had blown halfway to Lebanon County, but the trees were still having a storm of their own. Cleon and the mules and the tobacco wagon, with its load of long, wooden, backless benches, got a chilly shower with each breeze that chased after the rain clouds.

As he reined in alongside Henry Weaver's long back porch, he looked up to see Henry himself smiling from the shelter of the slate roof. Cleon nodded almost as curtly at Henry as he had at the man in the black car.

"You look like an old, wet rooster," Henry teased. Cleon didn't answer at once. The two of them began to untie the benches from the simple framework of the to- bacco wagon. They lowered one bench to the ground, righting it and dumping out water which had collected in the trough of the upside-down seat.

"Saw your cousin Joshua in his Chevvy. He splashed me."

"The Bible says. . . ."

"I know what the Bible says. Joshua oughta read it. Since he joined them Black Bumpers, he thinks he's smarter than us."

"He was always sort of for the Church Amish any- ways," Henry offered.

They stacked two benches and carried them toward the back door. The board supporting the seat of one bench displayed, in paintbrush lettering, the legend, "CLEON YODER 49." Some of the other benches bore similar

labels, to show who had made them and when.

As the two men carried the benches from the wagon to the wide parlor of Henry Weaver's house, they talked of Old Order or House Amish, which they were; and of the more liberal Church Amish, which many of their friends and relatives were; and of how some of their acquaintances had been falling away to other Plain Sects which permit the luxuries true Old Order Amishmen must not own.

For tomorrow was the Sabbath. Amishmen think of religion a great deal, but they go to worship only every other Sunday. Why? That's the way it's always been, as long as anybody can remember. Maybe it was different once. There are no records to tell, though. There are no written church records at all.

Births are penned on pages set aside for the purpose in the family Bibles. But that's about all any later generation will find of Amish church history written by Amishmen. Because of this, a change in congregational rules can become rigid church canon in the few years it takes the average person to forget things as they used to be.

At one time, certainly, House and Church Amish were one. About 1870, however, came the schism. Today they go separate ways. House Amish have services in the homes of the members. Their houses are so designed that folding doors can be shoved aside and the entire downstairs made into one big room. Members take turns being host to the congregation. Benches must be hauled from one house to the next during the two-week period between services.

Church Amish needn't bother with that. Their un-

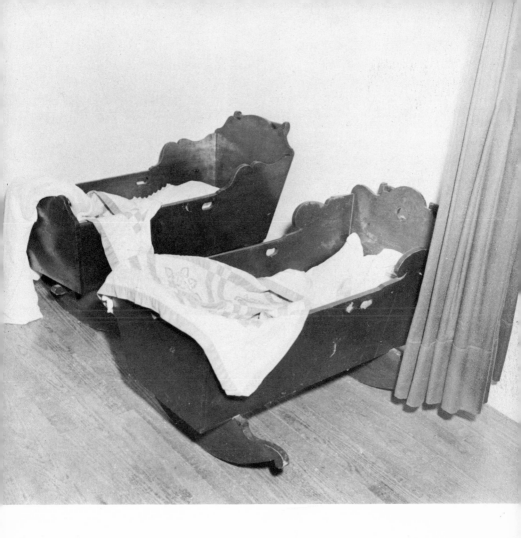

adorned places of worship, looking somewhat like Quaker meetinghouses, are innocent of stained glass or wall paintings or altarcloths or fancy carved pulpits. Everything is of Spartan simplicity. A center aisle divides the men from the women.

The only ornamentation you might find in an Amish church is in the small back room where the youngest babies are left. Here there are a couple of little wooden cradles with the typical broad Dutch heart carved through the headboards.

An Amish church has pews with backs, electric lights overhead, and even an electric clock right behind the preacher. An electric tube light aids the minister. The oldest members sit up front, on benches placed at right angles to the other pews and ranged against the front wall, facing the centered pulpit. These form the Amen Corners. In front of the pulpit, there is a small communion table, covered with common oilcloth. The rostrum, raised two steps above the flat church floor, is shellacked to a high shine.

Church Amish are permitted to own automobiles, though many of them do not, and those who do are careful to paint all the brightwork with a thick coat of dull black. They may even have telephones and electricity in their homes—but no radio or television.

Church Amish are inclined to look with some pity and occasional derision upon their old-fashioned kin, the Old Order or House Amish. However, there are a great many more House Amish than Church Amish in Lancaster County.

It is the Old Order which has held closest to the traditions of the group which split off from the original Mennonite faith (founded in 1632 by Menno Simon) to form, under the leadership of the seventeenth-century preacher, Jacob Amen, one of the myriad Protestant splinter sects. Many of the divisive forces of early Protestantism have disappeared and the schisms healed. But the Amish have survived, their doctrinal difference a sort of theological museum piece.

The Old Order Amish gathering for worship at Henry Weaver's house drove their buggies and wagons—perhaps 75 strong—up the lane well before the beginning of services at 8:30 A.M. Horses that couldn't be stabled in the barn were tied in a long row outside and the carriages parked in the field nearby.

Friends and family had helped shove aside the folding doors, and the men had placed the backless benches. Before the dew had dried on a million cobwebs polka-dotting the hay stubble, the women and girls ranged themselves on the left side of the house and the men and boys (except the youngest, who are allowed to remain with mother) on the right. Until the service started, the men kept their hats on.

Three hours of preaching in High German and hymn-singing in "Dutch" lay ahead as the first minister rose to open the service. Talking in relays, ministers and the bishop spoke on church matters, sermonized, and read from a big German Bible. The Amish use a Bible printed from old plates which they themselves own and lend to the local printer chosen to do the work. Binding is done out-of-town.

To start a hymn at an Amish service, one of the elders will rise, pull at his beard and hum until he hits the right pitch. Then he leads off.

When any church office is to be filled, a number of candidates are suggested by officers of the church and members of the congregation. At a service, they are all called to the front of the room, where there is a table on which rest as many Bibles as there are candidates. When all have Bibles, they are told to turn to a given text. The one who finds a slip of paper at that page is the new officer of the church. Amish believe that the Lord will in this way select the best man. Each congregation has a bishop, two preachers, and a deacon, all chosen by Biblical lot.

Children do not become church members until they have reached an age of discretion—which may be anywhere from 16 to 22, averaging about 18. One boy told of being rejected for membership because the bishop measured his hatbrim and found that it was only 3 ¼ inches wide instead of the prescribed 3 ½ inches.

It is at church service that the Amish are told of members who have misinterpreted or broken the rules. The worst punishment of all is excommunication or "miting." A mited Amishman cannot eat in the same room with others of the faith. They will not speak to him or do business with him. Since most of his friends are Amish, he will be a terribly lonely person until the churchmen relent or he breaks all church and family ties and starts a new life among the non-Amish. Few have the courage to risk the frightening penalty of the shunning.

Church officials who are too lenient face the stern censure of the older members. One Amish bishop who had been criticized for being too easy on the wild youngsters of the congregation was found hanged by a rope from a rafter of his barn. Relatives say he could not face the prospect of a visit by a group of the elders, who were scheduled to descend upon him the next day.

Anyone who wishes may join the Amish church, if he is willing to obey the rules. But there is no missionary work, no proselyting. The Amish are content to keep their own. A convert would be a prime curiosity.

Perhaps their success in keeping the membership growing from their own large families may be illuminated by a moment late that Sunday morning, a moment when the congregation were gathered up in a serene sense of belonging. One of the preachers at the Weaver home was preparing to administer the twice-a-year sacrament of Holy Communion.

Outdoors, the midsummer heat rose with the approach of noon. One of the horses tied to the barnyard fence neighed sharply, as another nipped at his flank. The trampled straw and mud and manure of the barnyard breathed a strong animal odor toward the house—an odor with which any Amishman feels comfortably at home. Indoors, where hall and parlor and sitting room had all been thrown together into a single low-ceilinged room, there was a teasing smell of chicken stewing with celery, in conflict with that of the fresh paint which Henry Weaver had hurriedly applied to peeling windowsills a few days before. The downstairs was pleasantly cool, despite strong sunlight filtering through curtained, but unshaded, windows.

Near the closed front door, one of the congregation's preachers rose to break in pieces a loaf of homemade bread, to pass to each member in turn the large china cup filled with wine, and to speak in German the words which give this stubbornly independent little church unity with all Christendom:

"This do in remembrance of Me. . . ."

AUGUST

There has been a revolution in the manufacture of cigars, but you will see little indication of change in the labor of an Amish family preparing to harvest its big cash crop of cigar tobacco in the waning heat of late August.

Lancaster has long been proud of its Type 41 Pennsylvania seed leaf. Some 90 per cent of the nation's acreage of this crop, traditionally used for cigar wrappers, is grown within the county. The Amish have made its culture an art.

Now the development of synthetic tobacco processes threatens the entire scheme of farming for thousands of prosperous raisers of tobacco. Briefly, the homogenizing results in a continuous ribbon of manufactured binder, which can be fed from spools into cigar-making machines. This apparently means that a premium price will no longer be paid for the finest Type 41 leaf. To the machine, all leaf will look the same—large or small, heavy or light, mosaic-marked or perfect. Stems, ribs, and leaf—all go into the vat and emerge in a smooth and flawless sheet at the other end of the line.

To the Amish, and to most other farmers of Lancaster, this will probably mean a tremendous change in the raising of tobacco, in the freewheeling purchase by field agents of tobacco companies, in the long hours of quiet cold-weather work inside the warm tobacco cellars. And the result in dollars and cents has not yet been ascertained. Cigar tobacco has paid into the pockets of Lancaster farmers an average of around $20,000,000 a year, so the new developments are being watched with care.

This year's crop on the Moses Riehl farm near Monterey is being harvested very much as Moses' father harvested his crops. Moses usually cuts his tobacco any time between the end of August and the end of September. Early frost has never yet caught him trying to squeeze a few hundred pounds' more weight onto his crop.

Moses Riehl, his wife, his three sons, and his three daughters all take part in the harvest. Tobacco is an all-year, all-ages business. It requires more man-hours of hand labor than almost any other farm product. That's why it is an ideal crop for the unmechanized, hard-working, patient Amish, with their many children to help them.

As soon as the sun has dried the dew from the great, drooping leaves (the smallest Riehl could hide behind the biggest tobacco leaf), Moses and the older boys are moving along the tailored rows of plants. One powerful snip of their long-handled tobacco shears cuts through the tough stem about four inches from the ground; the blade is angled so the plant will fall away from the standing row.

Methodically the cutters step from stalk to stalk. An

145

acre of tobacco is a fearsome sight to the city man thinking of hacking his way through it, but the Riehls planted
eight acres this year. They will cut it all within a couple
of days.

Quickly wilting in the heat, the windrows of tobacco
plants are left where they lie for half an hour to an hour
before the next operation.

If the sun is very hot, the farmer will watch his timing
carefully to prevent a "burn" which would give his tobacco a bitter taste.

Spearing comes next. That's a man's job, too, though
Mrs. Riehl and the older girl will help. A three-foot
wooden tobacco lath is capped with a sharp metal point,
and the thick stalk at the bottom of the cut plant is
speared with this weapon, the stalk then being slid onto
the lath. As each lath is filled with speared tobacco plants,
it is laid gently on the ground to await the coming of the
tobacco ladder. This is a long, narrow wagon bearing a
wooden frame wide enough so that the laths of tobacco
can be suspended from it high enough to swing the tips
of the hanging plants clear of the wagon body, free from
damage. Here a team of mules aids in a process which so
far has depended entirely on strong backs and dexterous
hands.

The Riehl tobacco shed and barn can hold about six
acres' crop of tobacco, hung from ceiling to floor, still on
the laths. (The metal spear point is removed and used on
succeeding laths.) Since there is just not room for all the
tobacco, some of it will be hung on high sawhorses in the
field near the barn—a risky business, for late summer

storms often knock these precarious frameworks down and ruin the leaf before it is dry enough to take indoors. If it survives, it will dry quickly and the tobacco can then be hung much closer in the barn, taking up less room than the freshly cut plants.

Tobacco sheds are built with slats in the sides which can be opened to give the drying leaf free circulation of air. Ordinarily the slats are vertical along the entire length of a barn, though in some barns they are horizontal. They make striking shadow patterns in the autumn sunlight.

As the crop cures, the leaf ribs will become dry and the leaves will take on the good, rich brown which the Amish like to duplicate in paint on their kitchen chairs. The tobacco bouquet is pleasant and powerful.

Lancaster's perverse climate helps Moses cure his tobacco. During the early part of November, the warm air will bring the high-hanging leaf to a hard and brittle state, but by the end of the month, the leaf will have started absorbing moisture again from the air, and become pliable.

When the tobacco has reached a state that Moses thinks workable, usually sometime in December, he and his family will take down the whole crop and store it in the tobacco cellar beneath the barn. Here the leaves will remain damp and easy to handle. Adjoining the cellar is the stripping room. Its narrow windows look out just at ground level. It is equipped with a small but hot-headed stove, a peg to hold a kerosene lantern, and slanting tables on two sides where the work is done. Such a room generally contains a bag of hoarhound lozenges and a jug of cider to cut the thick tobacco dust. (Lozenges are always "lozengers" in Lancaster County.)

Children too young for school will play in the stripping room during the long daylight hours while the parents work. This will go on through most of the winter months for the Riehls and their big crop.

Moses has stripped tobacco every winter for as long as he can remember. He could do it blindfolded. He'll carry an armload of laths loaded with tobacco from cellar to stripping room and remove the stalks one by one. Each leaf must be pulled separately from the stalk. When Moses has a goodly heap of stripped leaves, he'll begin sizing them. For this he uses a lengthing box, compartmented in six to eight divisions varying from 16 to 30 inches in length. Each leaf is fitted into its proper compartment. When a section is filled with leaves of a certain size, the leaves are removed and tied into a bundle with a smaller leaf.

Moses is happiest when he can tie up a "hand" of 30-inch leaf that's the right weight and texture, for these leaves are the "wrappers" used as the inside wrapping of the cigars—or they were before homogenizing was developed. Shade-grown Connecticut leaf has generally been used for outside wrappers. The big leaves have always brought the best price. The small leaves, and those with imperfections, become fillers for cigars, and are also bought for chewing tobacco, at much lower prices.

If Moses works a long day, from cow-milking in the morning to 9:00 at night, he can count as many as a hundred empty laths before he goes wearily to bed. His family will add to that number considerably, despite the time required for school and chores and cooking.

Moses may be uncertain on grammar, but there's nothing wrong with his arithmetic. He can tell you very quickly that this crop is averaging a pound and a half of stripped leaf per lath, and that the bales—which he packs himself in a hand-powered wooden baler—will weigh around seventy pounds, some a little more. He's been getting about three pounds of the more valuable wrappers to one pound of the cheaper fillers. And his crop should bring about $400 per acre when the buyers come around.

The buying of cigar tobacco in Lancaster County has been one of the few remaining areas of unrestricted free enterprise. It's a sparring match between the farmer and the various tobacco companies bidding for the crop. Each company has its own corps of agents. The rest of the year, these men (and an occasional woman) are salesmen, mechanics, preachers, store clerks, even farmers themselves. Each is an expert at guessing the value of an entire crop by examining the interior of one or two bales chosen at random.

Limits on what the buyers may offer are determined in very secret company meetings. A day and an hour are set for the simultaneous invasion of the field. Usually it is early in the morning, but you never know. Moses has his own friends among the buyers and prefers to deal with them. But he knows each buyer will make him only one offer. He'll say yes or no. If he sells too soon, it can cost him $500 to $1,000 by comparison with what he might get later. On the other hand, there is the possibility that full warehouses will mean a quick end to buying, and he will be left with the entire crop on his hands.

When the buyer offers him "28 and 10" (that is, 28 cents a pound for wrappers, 10 cents for fillers) and assures him that his Mennonite neighbor just sold a crop for that, Moses wonders whether there was any "bonus" payment that he hasn't been told about. It works this way:

In order to establish a lower price than the farmer wants to accept, a buyer may offer a generous bonus at the first place he visits. This will persuade his prospect to sell quickly, but won't be mentioned when the same price is offered to other farmers—without the added incentive. Books could be written about the tricks in the tobacco buyer's bag.

Usually the buyers will come up the lane before Moses has finished stripping his tobacco. Sometimes, however, when March arrives he'll still be peering through the dusty windows of the stripping room and wondering when the dickens they'll be there.

Moses knows a couple of tricks himself, but he doesn't use them. "It ain't honest. . . . And anyways you usually get caught," trying to slip a bunch of fillers into a bale that's supposed to be wrappers, or hauling in bales that have been permitted to soak up added moisture so they'll "weigh heavier." If you do get caught, your check will be held up until the whole crop has been examined by the buyer.

Usually Moses will say good-by to his crop when he hauls it to the company warehouse, where he waits calmly for hours in the long queue that includes horse-drawn wagons, tractors with wheeled flats, and huge truck vans.

By that time his next crop is already in the making. As a rule, he will have permitted half a dozen of the strongest tobacco stalks to go to seed. When the blossoms have turned to seed pods and ripened, these tops are cut and hung to dry; then the tiny seeds are cleaned out of the pods. If sold, they bring about $1.50 an ounce.

It's about the second week in March when Moses goes down to the cellar and picks out a dozen or more jars, fills them with tobacco seed, and sets them on the sills of all the sunny windows. The seed must be kept damp, and every child in the family must remember to discourage the killing mold by shaking the jars regularly until the first sprouts split the seed hulls. That will be around the first week in April, an exciting time on a tobacco-raising farm, for that is when the seedbeds must be steamed.

Just within the past half-century some rural genius discovered how to defeat the nemesis of seedbeds—weeds which crowded out the delicate young seedlings before they could get a good start. Live steam does the trick. It kills all weed seeds before the tobacco is planted. In Amish country, the tremendous, lumbering, old steam traction engines, with their iron wheels and their fancy trimmings and their strident whistles, do the steaming.

Custom steaming is done by small crews established at strategic intervals through the tobacco country. Around New Holland, a farmer will generally call on Jerry Overly for the job. In the Strasburg-Paradise area, it's likely to be Dick Hershey. Then there are a few Amishmen who serve their own people.

Long, narrow seedbeds are prepared by digging and

then raking again and again, until the soil is almost as fine as talcum. The ground must be dry to permit the steam to permeate it. A metal pan 14 feet long and 6 wide—the standard width of all seedbeds—is required. It has four sides and a top, with the bottom open. A large hose is attached in the center. The heavy pan is dropped in place over one end of the seedbed, and loose dirt is packed around it. The fire in the traction engine's boiler is stoked until the pressure gauge goes staggering into the higher figures, and then live steam is turned into the hose. The pan is left in place for twenty minutes to half an hour. By that time no weed seed within six inches of the surface can have survived. Then the pan is moved one length down the bed, the whole process being repeated over and over until the job is done.

One of the pleasures of the small boys who inevitably surround this operation is the bringing of a hatful of fresh eggs from the henhouse to the seedbed, where they are buried just before the steaming pan is tucked in. When it is moved to the next section of the seedbed, the youngsters leap into the hot loam to retrieve their hardboiled eggs.

During the season, the traction engine crews work around the clock. They present a scene from a witches' Sabbath on a moonless night when the red flames flash from the firebox and tint to pink the rising clouds of steam.

As soon as Farmer Riehl's tobacco bed is finished, the engine heads down the road at its top speed of two miles per hour. Every so often, its river-boat whistle whoops through the night, and neighbors for miles around awake and cuss mildly at being disturbed. According to such veteran experts as Clayton Overly of New Holland RD 1, however, the whistling is a signal that no real traction engine driver would omit. It's a tradition handed down from the early days of road-going machinery, when the law required blowing the whistle every hundred yards to warn other travelers that they'd better get well off the road, unless they wanted the gear-gnashing monster to scare their teams into a runaway.

Within six to ten hours after the rig has chugged away, Moses Riehl is ready to sow his sprouted seed. He rakes it gently and evenly into the pulverized soil, then covers the whole surface with tobacco muslin. Until the healthy seedlings appear above ground, the muslin is kept in place. Both before and after the seedlings appear, there must be constant watering of the beds.

It's close to Decoration Day (as Memorial Day is generally called in the country) before the young plants are ready for the field. In the meantime, the farmer has spent hours plowing, harrowing, disking, and rolling his acres, until there is not a clod the size of a nickel in sight. From above, the manicured soil presents a pattern of graceful scrolls where the horse-pulled roller has made its final evolutions.

All other work ends when tobacco planting begins on the Riehl farm, and all eight members of the family help. First the tender plants are pulled from the beds. Planks on each side of the bed hold another plank crosswise over the seedbed, and the people who pluck the plants must

balance on this board and lean down below it to reach the young sprouts. Though there are thousands of these tiny plants, they must be pulled one at a time, and with the greatest tenderness. They go into a shallow box about two feet square.

The tobacco planter consists of a pair of wheels and a driver's seat, a huge water barrel, and two low-slung seats just above ground level. The driver holds the horse to a slow walk. As the machine moves in a straight line up the field, it plows open two furrows four to six inches deep. Every two feet, there is a loud click and two squirts of water strike the soil. At each wet spot, the people on the low seats drop a tobacco plant. A board on the rear then closes the furrow around the plant. Straggling along behind will be one of the younger Riehls with a handful of spare plants to be stuck in where the planters have missed. Moses Riehl figures on planting maybe half of his eight acres in a single day's work.

For days after the planting, you'll see Moses walking the newly set rows and looking for seedlings sliced off by cutworms. These dead plants, he will replace. As the tobacco strengthens, Moses will give it a couple of spray treatments to discourage tobacco worms.

These tobacco worms are creatures which might throw most city women into screaming fits. They may be six or more inches long; they are horned, fat, green. Yet you'll see the smallest of the Riehl daughters among the maturing plants, picking worms off the leaves with her fingers and crushing them underfoot. And often it is a bare foot.

Cultivation removes some of the weeds, but tobacco must be hoed. Here again, the uninitiated will look at a couple of acres of tobacco and simply reject the idea that any family would be so crazy as to set out to chop a weeding-hoe into the soil around every plant. But it's all in a day's work to the Riehls.

If Moses Riehl saw the average field of cigarette tobacco in Maryland or Virginia, he'd come away with a very low opinion of the farmers there. For there seems to be no disgrace in letting cigarette tobacco go to seed. In Lancaster County, however, only half a dozen plants to a field may be allowed to blossom. The rest are topped, so that the growth will go into the leaf, where it counts on the tobacco company's check. Nearing maturity, the tobacco is suckered to nip off any remaining shoots from the main stem. These operations are entirely handwork. And for a long time after the suckering, the black of tobacco sap will stain the hands of those who helped do the job. It just has to wear off.

The one-room school to which the Riehl children go opens much earlier than nearby consolidated schools. It's in business by the middle of August. That's because the school directors know they'll have to dismiss all able-bodied youngsters for several weeks during the tobacco harvest.

People who don't know better may grumble at the way the Amish work their children. The fact is, the older boys need no slave-driving, because they know they will share in the cash return from the crop. There are other rewards for the younger ones. Most Amish toddlers look forward impatiently to the opportunity of working beside the older members of the family. They are taught responsibility rather than obedience. It's a great day when the little girl is first permitted to carry a handful of seedlings behind the planter, when the little boy is first handed the reins of the tobacco wagon.

Most Amishmen smoke cigars rather than cigarettes. A few roll their own. There is no anti-tobacco movement among the realistic Amish, and most of their "Plain" neighbors share their tolerance of the profitable weed, with the exception of a small group of Wengerites living in the countryside around Terre Hill and Blue Ball.

Now the tobacco farmer is being told that his pride in quality of leaf is becoming obsolete. In a few years quantity will be the only criterion, for the homogenizer doesn't care whether the tobacco it macerates has already been chewed up by a hailstorm or windowed by sun-scald. Perhaps the day will come in Lancaster County when the Amish will turn to another money crop. One Amishman, admittedly a little lazy, has anticipated this possibility by going into the business of raising chickens. "Chickens," he observed, "don't take no hoeing."

SEPTEMBER

Most experts on Amish life and customs would agree that there's little possibility of such a thing as an Amish rodeo. An Amishman treats his livestock with the same care and respect he accords other items of value. He doesn't show off. He's not competitive. All his training and discipline militate against an Amish boy's riding a good heifer around the barnyard to the hoots of his assembled friends.

But it has been known to happen. Usually it's in the warm of September, some weeks after a circus or a tent-show rodeo has played New Holland.

An Amish boy is not afraid of anything that neighs, moos, or bellows, and for a time there is a tyro bronco-buster behind every barn. The local physician and the osteopath, who has built a private hospital just outside town, have a rushing business in the setting of broken arms and collarbones. Amish girls boast to one another that "My Abram can ride a steer just as good as that fellow in the show." And pretty soon an Amish rodeo is being organized in a very quiet way.

It is held on a Sunday morning, when the congregation is gathered at a farmhouse safely hidden beyond a couple of hills. The word has been spread guardedly. Some of the more adventurous girls have been told they may attend. The teen-age ringleaders make their separate excuses for not attending services and turn up at the chosen farm for the big event. A few even have fancy saddles, ten-gallon hats, leather cowboy chaps, and spurs—the entire costume having been concealed in the attic or the barn until the right moment. Mostly, though, the headgear is broad-brimmed and black, and everyday clothes are worn.

Horses for the rodeo come hitched to the single-seat, open-top bachelor buggies. There may be a plowhorse and a mule for variety, but in the main the mounts are good horseflesh. Amishmen don't buy slow horses to pull their buggies, and many of these animals could trot a creditable turn ahead of a sulky on Roosevelt Raceway.

This particular rodeo has some unorthodox features. To begin with, there's a photographer present, summoned by an Amish youth who called him on the telephone. (The call was made from the booth in a small store popular with teen-age Amish boys.) One of the boys confides that they've been sternly forbidden to have a rodeo at all, because they had a rehearsal a couple of weeks ago and ruined several valuable milk cows. But they are having it anyhow, and what's more, some of them want their pictures taken in action—though the more conventional, or more timid, shy away from the camera. Assured the photographer is ready, they stage the Grand Entrance, cantering in, a dozen or more abreast, yippeeing and waving

their hats, while the comedian of the outfit—a youngster on a tiny jackass—capers along for laughs. All told, there are perhaps a hundred beardless boys and thirty-odd teen-age girls here to take part or to watch.

The barnyard becomes a corral. Fence rails rigged just inside the barn door to make a western-style chute hold the first uneasy heifer as she's cinched for riding. A lean-faced youth climbs onto the heifer's broad back, and a half dozen of his friends press around and yell and ring noisy cowbells and poke the heifer with pointed broom-sticks.

The gate swings open, and the frisky young cow leaps out, with her rider astride for as long as he can stick. A trip to the barnyard straw is the inevitable windup.

The bigger boys ride first. There's always a dispute as to who will be next. Some of the junior buckaroos are a little hesitant, but each one gives it a try.

Finally a mean old red bull that's been kept for the climax is trotted out of his stall toward the chute. With a snort, he breaks loose and in a moment has kicked down barriers and freed a whole flock of cows that moo with alarm and gallop round the inside of the barn. One of them crashes into the support for the tobacco hanging from floor to roof, and the heavy laths crumple in a cloud of brown dust and a splintering of wood and a chorus of yells, bovine and human.

For some moments, all is chaos. Brown tobacco dust pours from every door and window and crack in the barn. When the bull is at last confined to the chute and the cows are back in their stalls, the son of the farm's owner,

a little pale beneath the dirt on his face, mumbles, "I wonder how I'll explain that to Pop!"

But buoyed up by the spirit of the rodeo, he insists he's the man to ride the bull. Once he's athwart the sharp backbone, he lets out a yell and his friends let out the bull. Up in the air and down hard on all four feet goes the bull. Then his rear end shoots up like the free end of a catapult, and the erstwhile bulldogger somersaults through the air and winds up yards away. In an instant he's on his feet again, rubbing his shoulder and insisting it doesn't hurt, as his furious steed leaps the fence, rushes across the field, and disappears behind a neighbor's barn.

The show's not over. Cowboys generally rope calves; but this isn't the season for calves, so the Amish boys settle for goats as targets for their lariats. Some of these Blue Ball cowpokes are pretty good ropers, too.

Bronco-busting comes next, but the spirited horses are used to wild riding and refuse to get excited as an unbroken bronc should. However, there's a half-wild mule in the barn. He gets a chance to throw every Amish boy in the lot, and does so with dispatch. But they keep coming back, and finally, out of sheer exhaustion, the long-eared critter lets some of them stay in the saddle. About the only constructive result of this outing is one "well-broke mule," as the local newspaper ads put it.

There happens at this time to be a detour past the chosen farm, and cars line up on both sides of the black-top, as dozens of passers-by take advantage of the free show. Begun about 9:00 in the morning, the rodeo ends at 11:30, as the last of the animals plays out or runs away.

September

A week later, a picture story appears in the Lancaster *Sunday News*, and there's hell to pay at home. One of the boys, carrying a paper in his pocket to show to any friends who might have missed it, runs into the stern old bishop. Jerking the newspaper from the boy's pocket, the old man frowns at the hated photographs.

On the following Sunday, the young offenders are summoned to church. Every one of them is told he is expelled from the congregation. Parents, too, are warned: they must keep the photographer off their farms.

Being Amish, however, and notably softhearted where youngsters are concerned, their elders soon permit the sinners to return to the fold, after they've suitably confessed their guilt. The whole matter seems settled as thoroughly as the dust from the hundreds of dollars' worth of ruined tobacco in the rodeo barn.

The photographer is told of the decision to bar him from Amish homes. For a time he stays clear, but one evening he stops to pass the time of day with one of the older Amish fathers, and the whiskered patriarch smiles a greeting. After a little palaver, he turns to look out over the pasture and says wistfully:

"I chust wish you could get a picture of the old bishop and put that in the paper once!"

OCTOBER

This farm belongs to a bishop of the Old Order Amish church. On this starlit Saturday night, the great barn, two tobacco sheds, three-story chicken house, and 16-room stone home are a mass of solid geometrical shapes blocked against the horizon. An open buggy jogs toward the farm; the lively horse pricks his ears forward and steps a little faster. Ahead, around the barn in the darkness, there are already more than a hundred buggies like this one. The horses have been unhitched and stabled or tied loosely outdoors with some hay to keep them happy.

Tonight the bishop and his wife are not at home. As all wise Amish parents would do, they took the hint when their 18-year-old son announced he was having a dance at the barn, and they have long since hitched up and driven away to visit relatives for the week end. Tonight belongs to the young people. A Lancaster high school girl who learned the figures of the square dance at the City YWCA might not recognize this as a barn dance, if she happened to wander in. She probably wouldn't stay long enough to discover that here is a social event which has changed in only a few details since her great-grandparents met as these young Amish are doing tonight. It's not hard for an outsider to get into an Amish barn dance, but it is hard for him to stay. The invitation to leave is likely to be quick and unceremonious, for visitors are no more welcome than older Amish would be. There are no chaperones.

Inside the barn there hangs from a rafter a single gasoline lantern, its mantle glowing brightly. The harsh light picks out nearby cobwebs and casts gigantic shadows on the slate roof slanting as high above as a circus tent.

It is 10:30, and the three-piece band is clanging away with "Old Joe Clark." An Amish boy plays a fancy new guitar, and two non-Amish youths, one with a guitar and the other with a fiddle, help beat out the rhythm.

The boards on the floor are wide and rough where horses' hoofs and ironclad wagon wheels have hacked away at them for eighty years. Baled straw forms a wall along one side. Close-packed couples wheel in a rough version of a Paul Jones. The boys and girls here tonight are from 14 to 22 years old (after 22 there's not much hope for marriage), and there must be two hundred of them.

The non-Amish boys of the band—one wears a tucked-in sweater in a zigzag pattern, the other a black and white cowboy jacket—change the tune to "Lop-Eared Mule." Nobody calls figures for a square dance—no caller could be heard.

The noise rises sharply over near the twenty-foot-high double doors. Dancers mill away as the doors swing outward, and there is a chorus of maidenly screams as the lantern lights up a horse and buggy heading right into the crowd.

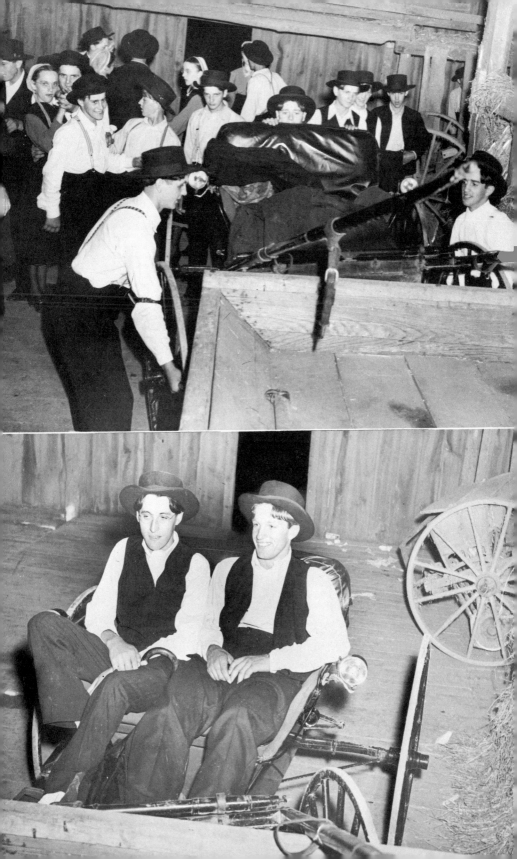

October

Two Amish boys and their girl friends, each one, except the driver, clinging to the rocking buggy seat with one hand and waving a bottle of beer in the air with the other, triumphantly circle the entire floor, scattering their yelling friends into safe, dark corners. Finally the driver hauls on the reins, the youngsters climb down, and the horse is unhitched and led away.

The buggy becomes a grandstand for anybody who's too exhausted or shy to dance. As body heat warms the vast air space, the boys haul off their coats and pitch them up on the bales of straw. Some keep on vests. Others strip down to shirt and suspenders. Shirt collars are all open. But the black hats stay on. So do the filmy prayer coverings of the girls, though their outdoor bonnets were removed as soon as they arrived.

In one corner a tall boy, whose face seems all bone and muscle, looks through eyelids narrowed by beer at the girl laughing up at him as they dance. His hand is pressed hard against the triangular black yoke which covers her shoulders. She holds a cigarette loosely, unfamiliarly.

Beer bottles are jammed into all available space in the milk cooler and the horse trough. Somehow, no matter how uncertain he may be on his feet, each boy manages to put his empties back in his own case, in his own carriage. It's understood that there will be no bottles left around the place. Sure, the old folks know what goes on at a barn dance. They did just about the same when they were courting. There's never been a custom more effective in the encouragement of early wedlock.

Bouncing along happily in the arms of a round-cheeked

boy, who holds her as if she were two plow-handles, is a little blonde hex who has had at least one partner for every dance. Standing tensely, alone, in the shadows by the wall, is another girl, built like a bed slat and scarcely past her fourteenth birthday, with an unchanging smile at the corners of her lips and the desperate hope in her heart that sooner or later somebody will grab her for a Paul Jones. Her wide eyes watch the dancers through gold-rimmed spectacles.

A surprising number of the girls wear glasses. In general, it doesn't seem to diminish their popularity. Among outsiders, there has long been a dispute as to the reason for this tendency in Amish girls and women. Have eight or ten generations of repeated inbreeding weakened their eyesight? Or do they fancy spectacles "just for pretty"— because they are not permitted any other kind of jewelry? If heredity's to blame, it seems largely to affect the distaff side.

Couples are continually coming and going through the small door cut in one of the big barn doors. Outside, there is the slap of a wagon-box lid closing, a giggle, and the fizz of a freshly uncapped bottle of beer. In many of the trunks built behind and under the buggy seats there are one or two cases of beer. On some of the seats silent pairs clutch and merge into single shadows.

Inside, the hillbilly tunes go on and on: "Arkansas Traveler," "Orange Blossom Special," "Mississippi Sawyer," "Ragtime Annie," "Rubber Dolly," "Chinese Breakdown," "Irish Washer Woman," "Fireball Mail." In the middle of "Boiling Cabbage Down," there's a yell and a scuffle and two boys wrestle out an argument in the haymow, while their girl friends stand by to cheer them on and other couples gather to watch.

Midnight passes, then 1:00, then 2:00.

Motes of dust shine in the brilliance around the lantern, and the dancers feel dust tingling on their sweating faces and in their nostrils. But farmers are used to dust, and they just open the big doors to the cool October air and keep dancing. Only the tenderest innocents have left the dance for home.

At a guess, perhaps half the dancers have been drinking. Most of them smoke cigarettes. One broad-shouldered young hulk announces, "I work hard all week and Saturday night I get drunk."

Somebody takes up a collection for the band, gathering the small coins in a wide-brimmed hat. The Amish are notoriously tightfisted, and the take is only a few dollars. But the musicians have been plied with all the beer they can hold, and they're not unhappy with their pay. By 2:30 nobody seems to know whether the orchestra is playing or not, and this includes the orchestra. About a third of the couples are dancing. Another third are in the haymow, fighting or watching a fight with equal concentration. The rest are outside in the pitch-darkness.

The Amish boy in the band suffers the only real tragedy of the night, when he lays down his new $125 guitar to go and dance and a horse steps clear through the instrument. But he goes back to play some more with an extra guitar one of the others brought along.

Some of the boys wander down into the tobacco-strip-

ping room below, where there's a poker game going on. This winter, when it's too cold to dance in the barn, the youngsters will organize a dance down there around the iron stove.

Along toward 4:00 in the morning, there's a general movement to break up the party and head for home. The boys who didn't feel obliged to kill half a case of beer start gathering up those who did. Horses are hitched to the proper buggies. Inert bodies are dumped on the seats, and a sharp slap starts each horse on his way, the empty bottles clinking gently.

Each sleeper will awake in his own barnyard, bleary-eyed but sadly certain of the unalterable fact that he's got a long day of hard farm labor ahead.

In a little while the wounds from haymow encounters will have healed, the deposits will have been collected on all the beer bottles, and the youngsters will be left to their memories until the word spreads that there's to be another barn dance, this time at Israel Kauffman's. With no telephones in their homes, how do they find out so fast? Well, there must be some secrets. Let's put it the way the bishop's son did, when he was asked. "What one Amishman knows, they all know."

NOVEMBER

Standing in the aromatic twilight of his cellar, Levi Beiler wondered suddenly if he would ever again be as happy as he was at this precise moment. Sure, the wedding was tomorrow. His first-born daughter would say the words that he and Annie had said 19 years before, almost to the day. It would be wonderful. Still, there would be so many people around, and he'd feel awful spited if he saw a straggly weed in one of the flowerbeds, or a streak of dirt on the sidewalk that one of the kids had missed. That wasn't likely, he knew. He had worked the five younger Beilers hard throughout the day, all around the yard and the farm buildings, making everything as neat and clean as Mrs. Beiler's kitchen. That kitchen! Today it wasn't safe for a man to get within yelling distance of it. There must be thirty women messing around up there, though what they were doing, he couldn't guess. Most of the food must be ready by now. In fact, here it was, on wooden tables and benches all around him in the cellar.

Levi turned slowly and started mentally to weigh and measure the quantities of food. He didn't have to count the chickens and ducks; he knew there were sixty of them, each cleaned perfectly and each with a quarter pound of butter lying on top, ready for the oven. Annie had said there'd be sixty pies, too, and there must be at least that many. Over there were three washtubs full of celery and a smaller tub with all the celery hearts—the last for the bride's table. The bride must have everything of the best. Those two lard cans were full of fresh applesauce. The cake table held eight five-pound fruit cakes, twenty layer cakes of wildly assorted flavors, and a tremendous wedding cake all done up with colored candies and nuts, that had been baked by the bride's younger sisters. Katie mustn't see this until she sat down to the wedding feast.

Then there were thirty large bowls of tapioca pudding and as many more of chocolate cornstarch pudding, a whole case of oranges, a full bunch of bananas, fifty two-quart jars of canned fruit, two cases of ginger ale, a wash-boiler full of chowchow, three washtubs of peeled potatoes, three lard cans filled with potato chips, and stacks of empty plates and platters and dishes on which the foods would be served. Levi felt just a little giddy as he tried to look at everything and separate the many odors from the pleasant, everyday cellar smell of the hard-packed earth on which he stood.

Probably few people alive today have ever seen as much home-prepared food as surrounded Levi Beiler on that day before the wedding. But there was lots more that he didn't see. Upstairs in the bustling kitchen the friends and relatives of the bride were still working on quantities of fresh bread, candies, jellies, sweet potatoes, fruits, peas,

beans, cheeses of many kinds, and the prize exhibit of the feast, the turkey which would grace the bride's table.

Annie Beiler worked with the rest, pausing only to shout to Levi to go out once to the tobacco shed and make sure the kids weren't fooling around with the hard cider and wine placed there to cool. Getting ready for the wedding was a big job. She'd had to make certain Levi's brother trimmed her husband's beard properly. And then Levi had gone around making sure the youngsters looked right. She chuckled as she remembered glancing out a window and seeing little Stevie tending the cow down by the fence while his father gave his small, bobbed head a fresh haircut on the spot.

Annie checked over the multitudinous details that every mother must remember the day before the wedding. Would there be plenty to eat? Invitations had been issued to 260 Amish adults—which meant heaven knows how many youngsters. Not engraved invitations, of course. Not even written. The Amish pass along these things by word of mouth.

This would be a Tuesday wedding. Most Amish weddings are on a Tuesday or a Thursday in November. Why those two days? There's church on Sunday, and that leaves Monday to get ready for a wedding on Tuesday; then Wednesday is free for catching up on work around the place, so everybody will be ready for another wedding on Thursday. Then there's Friday and Saturday to "get the work after" for church and a big dinner on Sunday.

And why November? November is an in-between month

on the farm. All the crops are in and stored for the winter, and it's not yet time to strip the still-drying tobacco. In fact, there's nothing much to do but get married, or at least help somebody else get married. Early in the month the Lancaster papers start carrying in their marriage license lists dozens of typical Amish names and addresses. Doctors of the New Holland area resign themselves to a heavy run of indigestion cases in bonnets and flat hats. Farm supply dealers prepare for a rush on all kinds of non-powered equipment, since a November marriage allows the young Amish pair a few months to make plans and preparations before starting farming in early spring.

Some of the couples will scout around for a farm they can operate on shares. That is, the owner bears half the cost of operation and splits the profits fifty-fifty. Out of their half, the young Amish will save all they can toward buying a farm of their own.

If they're lucky, newlyweds will be presented with a farm by the father of one or the other. It is customary to pass a farm along from father to son, but usually there is more than one son, so that the younger boys must look out for their own places.

On the wedding day, neither the father nor the mother of the bride is permitted to do a stroke of work. They are tended to almost as gently as the bride herself. At Beiler's there had been no rehearsals of the ceremony, no worry about flowers or trousseau. Actually, the Amish marriage is a simple rite, with none of the tulle and ribbons, none of the tail coats and carnations, of a non-Amish wedding.

The Amish regard the ceremony with such veneration

that it has never been photographed. Some pretty fabulous offers have been made for the opportunity, but local as well as outside magazine and news photographers have always been firmly turned away. Only close friends among the non-Amish are invited, and it's next to impossible for anybody else to get in.

Early on the morning of the Beiler wedding, the women were hard at work, cooking the meats and vegetables they had prepared the day before. The women who lived too far away to make the trip handily by horse and buggy had stayed overnight at the Beiler home.

Shortly after 7:00 A.M. the first guests began to drive up the lane.

With more than a hundred buggies and carriages expected, parking was a real problem. It was solved much as it would be at a society wedding in town. As each carriage pulled up to the front gate, one of the boys handed the driver a slip of paper on which a number was written. He wrote the same number in white chalk on the side of the wagon and again on the harness of the horse. Since each wagon looks exactly like every other one of the same model, the numbering is important. Other young men unhitched and stabled the horses and parked the carriages in a field near the barn. Late in the day, the driver would hand one of the boys his slip of paper, and the process would go into reverse, winding up in a short time with the right horse and buggy ready to go at the gate and the family loading up for the trip home.

The older married folks and the children entered by the front door, but the single girls went around to the back.

Clustered by the rear door were dozens of unmarried youths, who looked the girls over, as they tried to maintain their poise while running the gantlet of eyes, and mentally picked their partners for the evening's frolic.

By a quarter after eight all the guests were there, and the separation of the sexes began. With the entire first floor of the house opened up as for a church service, the women and children chose places on the wooden benches on one side, while the men settled down on the other. At 8:30 the three preachers who were to preside stood up at the front of the room. Men who still wore their broad-brimmed hats then took them off and carefully set them on the floor under the bench.

A wedding is one of the most solemn of all religious services, and for it texts dealing with the sacrament are chosen from the Amish Bible. At the Beiler wedding, some of the guests arose during the service and gave personal testimony, telling the bride and groom to be kind to one another.

For two hours, the preaching and the testimonies went on. Finally the preacher who would do the actual marrying got on his feet and started his sermon, which he concluded with the general invitation, "Now if there are any here wishing to be united in marriage, will they stand?"

After all the preparation, the marriage itself was plain, but impressive. The young couple, who had been sitting in the front row, arose. They were dressed no differently from any of the other young people. In a few simple words they were made man and wife, without a ring, without a veil, without a bridal bouquet.

It was half an hour before noon when the newlyweds were sent upstairs, out of sight, so the bridal table could be set. Children were shooed outdoors, and while the women headed for the kitchen, the men stacked the long benches on which they had been sitting, to make one great table extending the length of the house. The rest of the benches were moved alongside, to be sat on during the feast. Quickly the women set the table. Off to one side, the bride's table was prepared under the special care of her sisters and other girls close to her. On this table were placed many dainties not found on the big table, including the huge, brown-roasted turkey and the handsome wedding cake.

Brothers, sisters, and close friends sat down with the bride and groom when they were finally allowed to descend the stairs and see the marvels set out in their honor. There weren't enough places for all the other guests to eat at once, so all the men and some of the children sat down first. When they'd wiped the last crumbs from beards and chins, the women and the rest of the children filed in for their share. Afterward the tables were cleared of food, but left in place for the evening meal.

It didn't seem possible that any of the diners would be able to move, but they did. The children went outdoors again to play. The older men gathered near the barn for some man-talk, and the beardless boys watched for a chance to snatch the groom away from his bride. With much shouting, they grabbed him, hustled him to a board fence, and took a firm grip on hands and shoulders, legs and feet. With a swing and a heave ho, they chucked him

over the fence and into the waiting arms of the married men. It's an obvious bit of symbolism, tossing the groom out of the society of single men and into the fraternity of the benedicts.

One of the Beiler bedrooms had been set aside for a display of wedding presents. Tables ranged around three sides of the room were covered with gifts, and many more presents were heaped on the floor under the tables. Their quantity corresponded with the impressive number of guests, but few could have cost more than a couple of dollars at the general store. Everything was useful. Much was homemade.

Duplications of the usual variety—three waffle irons, four coffee urns—did not worry this young couple. Of course, they knew they would receive no electrical appliances, and any present that might turn up more than once was welcome. For example, no non-Amish bride in Lancaster County could expect to get one third the number and variety of dishes displayed here. Tableware came in dozens—varied plates, cups, and saucers, and an assortment of bowls and tumblers that would have done credit to the counters of Zimmerman's store at Intercourse. Amish people entertain on a grand scale, and there can never be too much china and glass and kitchenware in the house. There were cookie jars of all sizes and colors, numerous kettles and pots and pans and skillets, sets of stainless-steel knives and forks. (Silverware is seldom seen in an Amish household; cheaper ware is quite as serviceable and not so pretentious.)

Tablecloths ranged from linen to oilcloth. Thousands

of hours of handwork must have gone into the embroidered bedspreads, the bureau scarfs, the hooked and braided rugs of brilliant colors, the fancy cushions, even the humble little pot-holders.

There were "store-bought" blankets in profusion, too, though later the Amishwomen of the community would expect to be invited to a quilting party at the new bride's home to help her make some pretty coverlets.

Another kind of imaginative handicraft was to be found among the gifts. A number of large glass jars, of the sort in which restaurants buy pickles, had been painted with bright little country scenes. One of them was meant for a sugar jar, and on it appeared a red brick farmhouse, with the windows left clear so the bride could see when the sugar was running low.

It's customary for the older folks to head for home by four o'clock. That's how it was at Beiler's. The younger ones stayed on for the evening fun. They paired up and gathered around the tables again, finding them set with fruits and candies, hard cider and wine. After supper some started to sing. Others stood and talked. Others played old parlor games. The boys joked with the bridegroom about trading his bachelor buggy for a sedate family wagon, and about remembering not to trim his sprouting little beard tomorrow. (Amish young men actually start letting their chin whiskers grow when they become church members. As an old Amishman explained, "They don't have beards yet until they're married, but they don't shave neither.")

The girls, perhaps, reminded the bride to put away her

maidenly white apron and don the wedded woman's black.

It was a quiet, happy scene out of an idealized past. These youngsters, it seemed, could not be the same young roughnecks who would raise cain at a barn dance, with its unconfined rowdiness and close-to-the-surface sex.

On that same evening, as on many another, hundreds of young Amish were going through the classic pattern of courtship, which has worked out so very practically. They drive in from the country in their open buggies to the crossroads at Intercourse Village. Some boys have dates, but others bring their own undated sisters, exchanging them for other fellows' sisters in trading as shrewd as any you'd see at the New Holland Sales Stables. Bargaining is circumspect, but every boy knows the perils of getting stuck for the evening with a dumkopf (square) or an ugly one. Some have marriage in mind, and are looking for somebody "fer shteady." Others, playing the field, will settle for a pretty girl "chust fer so." An Amish boy with two sisters is assured of popularity.

As the pairing continues, couples drive off into the night in the open-top buggies. Automobile drivers familiar with Pennsylvania Route 340 can recognize a buggy a mile away by its bright but yellowish head lamps or the peculiar motion of the taillights, which are really just red glass behind the headlights mounted on the side. The comparatively slow progress of the buggies makes them a hazard in traffic.

Probably the young folks in the carriages say pretty much the same things as are being said in the convertibles

and jalopies which swing past them in the night, even if it is said in Pennsylvania Dutch.

A few years ago, the youngsters got so rambunctious that the good burghers of Intercourse called the cops. They complained to the County Detective and the State Police that the racket and confusion on Saturday and Sunday nights were getting to be just too much. One Sunday evening, a detail of State Police moved in. As the prosecuting officer said later, he was walking across the street at the intersection, when a bunch of buggies started to swing around him in a circle and he was hard put to it to avoid being knocked down and trampled under the hoofs. He was angry enough to collar four of the boys and haul them before a justice of the peace for fines and costs that ran to more than $18 apiece. They got a lecture as well and promised to behave in the future. Each produced a fat wallet to pay his fine.

Some people at Intercourse claimed the police picked a poor night, when there were only about a hundred buggies in town, compared with the usual two to three hundred. Complainants said buggy-racing on the streets and the highways nearby continued from nine o'clock at night until three in the morning, that some of the young folks drank beer and hollered insults at passing motorists. Whatever conditions may have been, they improved considerably after the arrests and the attendant publicity, which is in general detested by all good Amishmen. The courting assemblies continue, however, even if less noisily than before.

If a boy and girl like each other, they may decide to

get married, but it's always a dark secret from all their friends. The boy will go to a deacon of the congregation, who in turn will go to the girl's father and ask his consent for the marriage.

The father seldom refuses. The deacon then will take it upon himself to advise the young people on how to go about getting married. No Amish youth will admit he's engaged until his name appears with his fiancee's in the marriage-license column.

Eighteen is considered a good marriageable age, though some are wed as young as 16 and 17. Those not married off before 24 are considered well on the way to the unenviable state of bachelor or old maid. Neither is common among the Amish.

DECEMBER

Christmas comes twice a year to the happy Amish children. Second Christmas, December 26, is just as wonderful a day for Danny and Hannah Smucker as the great day itself. In their horse-paced community, it's not possible to stretch one holiday over all the friends-and-family celebrating. Danny and his sister are pupils in the first and second grades, respectively, of an Amish parochial school—which is overshadowed by a $2,000,000 consolidated high school spread across the top of a hill a few rods away.

The school the Smuckers attend was, up until a few years ago, a typical "little red schoolhouse," part of the township's system of education. There were 14 others that resembled it in its one-room size, its seventy-year-old brick construction, its coal-scuttle heating, its twin outhouses, the clang of its mellow old bell. Today all those old schools have been sold by the district. Some have been converted into snug homes, others have become tool sheds on the farms of families whose ancestors donated the ground "forever" for school purposes but thriftily reserved the right to take it back if school didn't keep. A few were bought by the Amish to establish their own schools.

This is a recent development. Most Amish youngsters still attend public schools. There they learn the gaiety of some of the Christmas customs which their people abandoned to less strict German settlers many generations ago. They sing "Jingle Bells" and "Up on the Housetop" as well as the newer numbers, such as "Rudolph the Red-Nosed Reindeer." They scissor Christmas trees from green construction paper and industriously paste on bits of tinsel and foil. They help build sandbox Christmas-tree lands, laughing at the farm scenes peopled by brightly painted Amish figures cast in iron by the Hubley Toy Company in nearby Lancaster.

In the famous Beiler school, whose pupils are mostly Amish, the beloved non-Amish teacher was presented a few years ago with a surprise Christmas gift. It was a white quilt on which each of the pupils' names was embroidered, together with quaint little figures of a schoolhouse, trees, flowers, and other designs. Most of the girls had stitched on their own names, and the mothers of the boys and of the youngest girls had put their names on for them. They were grouped by families, as many as three and four names together. This school has become well known to Amish-country visitors as a regular stop on the Hotel Brunswick's "Pennsylvania Dutch Week-end" bus tours.

What the visitors do not realize is the continued effort on the part of the Amish to bring up their children with

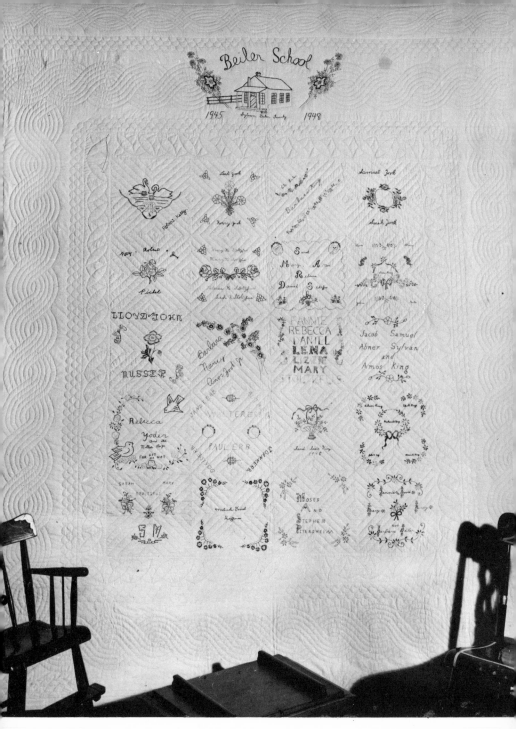

as little outside influence as possible. The move to paro-chial schools stems from this, as did the "passive resist-ance" campaign against sending children over 14 past the eighth grade—a campaign which has just ended in quali-fied victory for the Amish, after more than twenty years of what their defenders call persecution.

Sporadically the boards of school directors in districts which contain Amish would bring legal action against all parents who refused to send their 14-year-old boys and girls to school after they had completed the traditional eight grades of elementary education. Spokesmen for the Amish patiently explained many times, when given a chance at hearings, that they felt that from 14 on, Amish children could be better educated as farmers and house-wives on the farm and in the home rather than at school.

Legally, the children could have been relieved from school attendance if their parents had signed statements of dire need. But this the Amish, always comfortably situated, scorned to do. Amish are law-abiding. But they do not hesitate to defy a regulation which they feel is forcing them to betray their own beliefs.

Finally the State Department of Public Instruction brought pressure to bear on local school boards to en-force truancy laws. Publicity was given to the warning that districts which failed to enforce all such portions of the school code would not be granted their state subsidies. In many cases these subsidies represent a good portion of the budget, and so school boards, often reluctantly, put their truant officers to work. Prosecutions were brought against Amish parents whose 14-year-olds were staying away from high school. Offices of country justices were jammed to the doors—some of the accused stood on porches outside and listened through the window—as case after case was quickly settled. The Amish, of course, were almost always adjudged guilty. But they refused to pay their fines. This, they said, would be an admission of wrongdoing. Many went to county jail. Sentences varied from 24 hours up to several days for repeated offenses. Then Lancaster lawyers started appearing at the offices of the justices of the peace. Suddenly fines were being paid. It was always announced that the money had been contributed by a "good Samaritan," a friend of the Amish. Actually the fines were paid from funds collected among the Amish themselves. They were unobtrusively taking care of their own, just as they did during Depression days, when no Amishman ever appeared on the relief rolls.

As a test, one Amish truancy case was appealed clear up to the State Supreme Court. No decision was ever handed down. A new Governor, George M. Leader, who had promised to clear up the situation, finally got results. After many months of legal consultation and conferences between officials and an Amish educational committee, his Secretary of Public Instruction announced a new set of regulations. It immediately ended all prosecutions of Amish parents for truancy of 14-year-olds. It also raised a howl of protest from many Lancaster educators.

For the new plan, while not mentioning the Amish by name, permits any religious group to withdraw children from regular schools at 14 and continue their education at home. Five days a week parents, or those with whom the children are living, must see that they are trained in domestic and agricultural knowledge. They must keep nominal records of progress in case a state inspector stops by. And one day a week there must be an organized class in which English and arithmetic are taught. For the Amish, this one day is Saturday. School is in session from 9:00 A.M. to noon, under the tutelage of a young Amish preacher. The Amish Bible is part of the course of instruction. Several of these "schools" have been organized, all in unused portions of ample Amish farmhouses.

Some educators say three hours' school a week is no school at all. They claim that the new code represents a surrender which could lead to a widespread breakdown of the carefully built school system of Pennsylvania. They say the whole business was simply vote-hunting politics. It should be remembered, however, that the Amish don't vote except where they are directly affected. They have been known to register and vote in large numbers on issues that involved them personally: to elect a school director favorable to their views, or to keep out beer and liquor. Seldom do they vote in state and national elections. This is a reflection of their general lack of interest in things beyond their own families, their own farms, their own congregations, their own pocketbooks, their own convictions.

They ignore national holidays and the birthdays of heroes. Their holidays are religious holidays, and on these holidays no work is done. Twice a year, on Good Friday and early in October, they have fast days. That is, they

eat no breakfast—a tremendous sacrifice for an Amish-man. Dinner (at noon) and supper are the same as usual on these two days of preparation for communion. Communion takes place on the Sunday following the day of fasting and prayer.

Eastertime brings the most important group of holidays. In addition to Good Friday and Easter Day, there is Easter Monday, which, like Second Christmas, is an extension of the celebration. Forty days after Easter the Amish again knock off work for Ascension Day. For people in Lancaster City whose calendars do not indicate this day it is always unmistakable, for the Amish traditionally come to town in large numbers on Ascension Day.

Then comes Whitsunday, the eleventh Sunday after Easter, the day of Pentecost. Amish also call this day by its old English name of Whitsuntide. They continue in the spirit of two holidays being better than one by celebrating Whitmonday as well.

Thanksgiving is generally observed among the Amish. They may have church that day "if it suits," as an ancient Amishman expressed it. New Year's Day is another Amish church holiday. But that is all.

Even Christmas, a joyous time, is kept as simple and unadorned as the boxful of straw on which a star shone in Bethlehem.

In the Smucker home there is no Christmas tree. There are no holly wreaths, no electric trains, no colored lights. Danny and Hannah know of these things, of course. They visit shyly in the homes of friends, see their gifts, hear their talk. Perhaps they envy their non-Amish playmates momentarily.

Then, the day before Christmas, school closes early in the afternoon. Lancaster County frequently has weather that's distressingly warm right through December. That's why, as Danny and Hannah and their friends rush out the front door of their eight-grade school, they look up expectantly at the dark clouds scooting low over the pointed belfry, and ponder whether it's going to snow. In every barn there's a yet-unused sleigh. Impatiently they struggle into heavy rubbers or galoshes, which have been lined up across the front porch of the school like crows on a wire. Several buggies pull into the muddy schoolyard, and the youngest children are scooped inside. The others troop off in two jiggling lines in opposite directions along the road, guarded by some of the older children who have been appointed as safety patrols. Though the Amish may not drive cars, the State Police and Auto Club representatives are careful to include them in the safety program. An Amish boy from Lancaster County (Daniel Stoltzfoos, who in 1947 saved a girl from being hit by a truck) was one of the honored few to be greeted by the Vice President of the United States and personally commended for heroism.

On the day before Christmas a child, Amish or not, could have thoughts of only one thing. In the homeward procession pigtails may be pulled, books jostled, hats knocked askew. At lanes and at brown-hedged front yards, the children turn off by ones and groups. At last Hannah and Danny mount the foot-worn limestone steps of their own porch—a porch in the old tradition, a porch that starts over the front door and extends clear around to the back. There's a small rumble of running feet, quick thuds of discarded overshoes, an opening door, and Hannah and Danny are inside the sheltering arms of home.

Hannah's school clothes are a miniature replica of what her mother wears about the house. And little Danny is his father seen through the wrong end of a telescope—without the softly curling brown whiskers, of course.

In the warmth of a kitchen bigger than the whole floor space of any ranch house in the proliferating developments around Lancaster, the children are received into such a security of love and family unity and group tradition as today's hasty civilization does not offer elsewhere. Forgotten are the mechanical Santas, the jittery lights on Christmas trees already a month away from their Canadian stumps, the store-bought toys of which other children dream. Danny and Hannah are home. They are enveloped in a featherbed of Amishness. Shut away from the world, supremely happy in a household where there is seldom an angry word spoken, they know too well the good things of their way of living to be jealous of any other. The Amish way is their way. It has been from birth, it will be through the secret excitements of courtship and the solemn rite of baptism. It will be till death.

Before a hearty supper, well weighted on the side of protein and starch, there is the blessing of the meal. Before an early bedtime there is the reading of the Bible. All this is as natural as the coming of evening to the little boy and girl. Still young enough to sleep together in a wide old brass bed, under a comforter and a brightly geometrical patchwork quilt which their mother's friends

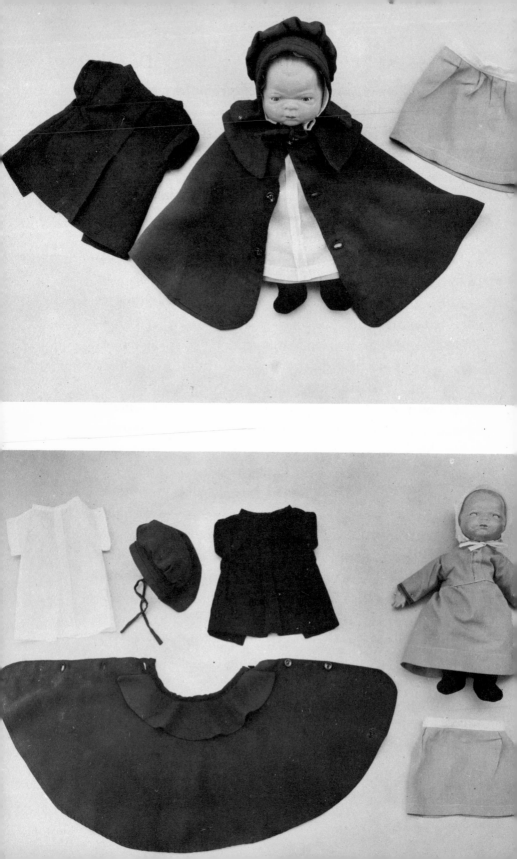

stitched when she was married, Danny and Hannah talk as any youngsters would on Christmas Eve. They have some ideas about the special cookies which have been baking while they were at school, though only spicy aromas in the kitchen corners remain as a hint of the varied flavors. They guess at their gifts. Hannah hopes that Grandma will have for her one of those rare rag dolls she can make, with a complete wardrobe of Amish girl's clothes. Danny figures on a practical quilted jacket like Pop's, but wonders secretly if his father might not just possibly have been fabricating a roller-skate scooter back in the barn.

Danny's milkweed-silk hair spreads across the pillow and his eyes shut. Hannah's unwound plaits flop gently around her pink-and-white face as she turns in a last conscious movement. Minutes later Mother comes quietly through the door and picks up the softly shining kerosene lamp. She lingers to straighten the quilt. There is a muffled thud of wood against the doorframe downstairs, and a slight click of metal, which could have come from a man's clumsy handling of something he was bringing in from the barn. A glance shows the sound has not disturbed the new sleep of the youngsters. The lamp's glimmer touches the unadorned walls, is absorbed in the black of the woman's skirt and apron, shines dully on the holly-green of her high-necked, long-sleeved blouse, illuminates a slight smile before the full lips pucker and puff out the flame.